ON BEING AN INTROVERT OR HIGHLY SENSITIVE PERSON

by the same author

Highly Sensitive People in an Insensitive World
How to Create a Happy Life
ISBN 978 1 78592 066 0
eISBN 978 1 78450 324 6

Come Closer
On love and self-protection
ISBN 978 1 78592 297 8
eISBN 978 1 78450 603 2

Tools for Helpful Souls
Especially for highly sensitive people who provide help either
on a professional or private level
ISBN 978 1 78592 296 1
eISBN 978 1 78450 599 8

The Emotional Compass
How to Think Better about Your Feelings
ISBN 978 1 78592 127 8
eISBN 978 1 78450 392 5

ON BEING AN INTROVERT OR HIGHLY SENSITIVE PERSON

A guide to boundaries, joy, and meaning

ILSE SAND

Jessica Kingsley *Publishers*
London and Philadelphia

First published by Forlaget Ammentorp, Denmark, in 2017
English language edition first published in 2018
by Jessica Kingsley Publishers
73 Collier Street
London N1 9BE, UK
and
400 Market Street, Suite 400
Philadelphia, PA 19106, USA

www.jkp.com

Library of Congress Cataloging in Publication Data
Names: Sand, Ilse, author.
Title: On being an introvert or highly sensitive person : a guide to
    boundaries, joy, and meaning / Ilse Sand.
Description: London ; Philadelphia : Jessica Kingsley Publishers, 2018. |
    Includes bibliographical references.
Identifiers: LCCN 2017059784 | ISBN 9781785924859
Subjects: LCSH: Introversion. | Sensitivity (Personality trait) | Introverts.
Classification: LCC BF698.35.I59 S26 2018 | DDC 155.2/32--
dc23 LC record available at https://lccn.loc.gov/2017059784

British Library Cataloguing in Publication Data
A CIP catalogue record for this book is available from the British Library

ISBN 978 1 78592 485 9
eISBN 978 1 78450 871 5

Printed and bound in Great Britain

CONTENTS

PREFACE

My first book, *Highly Sensitive People in an Insensitive World: How to Create a Happy Life*, was published for the first time in 2010 and has become a bestseller in a number of countries.

Since then, I have listened to many highly sensitive people and introverts in my practice as a psychotherapist and when I have held lectures on the subject. They have told me about their challenges, and I have advised them on the strategies that can be used in different situations. And as an introvert and a highly sensitive person, I have also gained new personal insights that I share in this book.

This book is written for highly sensitive people and introverts. However, its advice and instructions are also quite applicable to people who are, temporarily or for some other reason, in a sensitive situation – for example, because of stress, trauma, or burn-out.

The first chapter describes the introverted personality type, the highly sensitive trait, and the high-reactive temperament.

The following chapters contain good advice and concrete suggestions for how to set boundaries, protect yourself against over-stimulation, stand up for yourself, enjoy the company of others in your own way, and find joy and meaning.

At the conclusion of the book, you will find two self-tests to give you an idea of how introverted or sensitive you are.

People are very different, and no one fits 100 per cent into the description of a particular type. You will probably be able to recognise yourself in some parts of the description, while other parts will seem alien to you. You may also find that you benefit from the book's advice and instructions even if you do not think you fit entirely into any of the types.

I have tried to write the book in simple, easily understandable language without superfluous information.

The specific examples I use have, for the most part, been partially fictionalised for educational purposes. They contain typical situations and remarks I have heard over many years in my work as a parish pastor and, later, as a psychotherapist. Some of the examples are authentic. They have been used and made anonymous with the permission of the person concerned.

When I use the word 'extrovert' in this book, I mean it precisely in the sense first described by C.G. Jung. When the American psychologist and researcher Elaine Aron uses the term 'highly sensitive, socially extrovert', she does not mean exactly the same thing. All highly sensitive people possess a great deal of introversion. I shall elaborate on this in Chapter 1.

Introduction

I am so pleased to see how it has become more and more accepted and legitimate in recent years to be an introvert or a highly sensitive person. It was not always this way.

My grandfather, 'Planter Sand', came to Tversted – a dune plantation in the northern-most part of Denmark – in 1946. He landscaped the Tversted lakes, built paths and bridges, put up benches, and made the place into a popular excursion site. He was an extrovert and could hardly take a walk down to the lakes without meeting someone he fell into conversation with and invited home. It was important to him that everyone felt welcome to drop by the caretaker's house, which was close to the lakes, for a cup of coffee or to borrow the telephone. Many people availed themselves of the hospitality – including acquaintances who had summerhouses in the nearby town of Skiveren.

My grandmother was an introvert. Among people she did not know well, she was quiet and reticent. I remember that she had a very special relationship with her chickens. I still recall how she spoke to them in a bird language as she entered the chicken coop, creating an atmosphere of harmony and intimacy. When surprise guests came to the caretaker's residence, you could see how artificial her smile was. Once, just as she was absorbed in washing the dishes, clad in a filthy apron with her hair in a mess, the former Prime Minister of Denmark Jens Otto Krag suddenly appeared in the living room. My grandfather, of course, was delighted by the distinguished visit, while my grandmother smiled her artificial smile.

We all admired my grandfather. He was someone people noticed – in part, because on many occasions he gladly rose to give a speech – and he had something nice to say to everyone. His desire for company was easily aroused, and his ability to make contact with strangers was formidable. My grandmother, on the other hand, we often viewed as sad and negative. Over the years, she was tormented more and more by arthritis and, at the end, could not even turn her head. She had to live a completely different life from the one she wanted and had the talent for. It was too bad that none of us could see and recognise how hard she struggled to survive in an environment in which she was forced into far more sociability than she had the desire or energy for.

My grandfather was interested in the church and, for many years, was the head of the local church council in Tversted. Therefore, it was an important event for him when I got my first parish. He travelled down to Djursland with good ideas – for example, about how I could set up benches in the parsonage garden so the congregation could go for walks and enjoy sitting and gossiping on the benches. Instead, I put up a picket fence between the garden and the churchyard. I am an introvert and wanted my garden in peace.

When I applied for a job as parish pastor in Djursland, I had not realised that I was an introvert. But I discovered quickly that the expectations of how extroverted I was supposed to be in the parish were beyond my abilities.

I had replaced a pastor who had the habit of turning up unannounced on major birthdays, saying, 'Hello, it's the vicar. Happy birthday.' The complaints that I did not do the same came quickly. But, for me, turning up unannounced was far too great a challenge. If I drop into festive company I do not know, I become awkward and stiff – and before I have even turned around, I have used up my energy resources for several days. Even though I put together grief support groups and made much of pastoral care, nevertheless there were remarks about how I did not participate in the birthday of this person or that person throughout my years at the parish.

It was a gift for me to discover the concept of introversion. I now understood that I was neither lazy nor wrong: I was an introvert, and my talents lay elsewhere. This new knowledge gave me self-confidence and helped give me the courage to leave my civil-servant position as a parish pastor and step into new and untried pastures as an independent psychotherapist.

After I read the description of highly sensitive people by American psychologist Elaine Aron, I found that it supplemented my understanding of myself as an introvert, so that I became even clearer to myself. My shame at being different again diminished. It was good to know there were others like me – and I became convinced that those who had seen me as whining, self-absorbed, selfish, or lazy had viewed me wrongly.

Later, it became my mission to help others to have greater faith in themselves by learning about their personality type, to come to terms with their weaknesses, and to recognise their strengths.

Now I hope that this book may be a help for introverts and highly sensitive people who are even today sometimes viewed as grumpy or arrogant, for example when they take the time they need to compose themselves.

Chapter 1

Personality Types

When you divide people into types, it is important to remember that nobody fits 100 per cent into the description of a particular type. Every human being is far more than his or her type, and every human being is capable of developing over the course of a lifetime.

With that said, it can be helpful to find and come to know your own type and understand yourself and other people better. When you read about other types that are different from you, you realise how many different ways there are to exist in the world. You become aware that, when other people react differently than you would have done, it need not be because there is something wrong with that person or yourself. Both of you are okay as you are, but you belong to different types.

In the following sections, I shall describe the introverted personality type, the highly sensitive trait, and the high-reactive temperament.

The introverted personality type

The Swiss psychiatrist C.G. Jung provided a comprehensive description of the introverted and extroverted personality types for the first time in 1921. Since then, various studies have reached different numbers as to how many introverted persons there are. The results vary. They show that introverts constitute anywhere from 30 per cent to 50 per cent of the population.

Below is a series of statements that can give you an idea of where you belong.

IF YOU ARE AN INTROVERT, YOU WILL PROBABLY
ANSWER NO TO MOST OF THE STATEMENTS BELOW

~ I think a weekend without a party is a bad weekend, and I feel disappointed on Sunday evening.

~ I like knowing a little about everything, but if I have to dig more deeply into a particular topic for an extended period of time, I get bored.

~ I love excitement and throw myself gladly into new experiences without any major reflection.

~ I think best while I'm talking.

~ I do a lot to keep myself from being bored and try to have too many rather than too few appointments or activities on my calendar.

ON THE OTHER HAND, YOU WILL PROBABLY ANSWER
YES TO MOST OF THE FOLLOWING STATEMENTS

~ If I have to say something to a larger group, I prefer to be well-prepared.

~ If my own experience of what is true and correct conflicts with the general understanding of what is good, I am inclined to listen more to my own logic or intuition.

~ Others have told me that I think too much about things.

~ I am selective about the company I keep. In some contexts and with certain people, I enjoy being with others very much, but otherwise I prefer being alone to being with others.

~ If there is too much going on around me, I get tired and prefer to rest alone in peace and quiet or, perhaps, with a single person I know well.

At the conclusion of the book, you can find a comprehensive self-test that can give you a number for where you lie on the scale between introversion and extroversion.

A continuum

Introvert or extrovert: It is not an either/or. You can be more or less one or the other. On the scale below, you can place yourself about where you think you

belong on the scale at this point. At the conclusion of
the book, you will get a chance to chart a new scale.

```
 −60  −50  −40  −30  −20  −10   0   10   20   30   40   50   60
├──┼──┼──┼──┼──┼──┼──┼──┼──┼──┼──┼──┼──┤
Extrovert                    Ambivert                    Introvert
```

Some people find themselves in the middle. They are
called ambiverts. No one is 100 per cent introvert or
extrovert. Any such person would be insane, wrote
C.G. Jung. We all find ourselves somewhere on the
continuum, which means that we all have something
of the extrovert and something of the introvert in
our personality.

Where you would place yourself will probably
be different on different days or at different times in
your life. If you take a test several times at different
time points, you may find that the results vary – albeit
rarely from one extreme to the other. However, if you
find yourself most of the time at the introverted end of
the scale, you might move, for example, from being a
middling introvert to being very introverted depending
on how your life is shaping up at the moment.

Even though you are an introvert, you are undoubtedly
capable of acting in the world in an extroverted way
when you need to. But if it goes on for an extended
period of time, you will probably be tired afterwards.

Introverts typically do not care very much for
superficial interactions, like Lars in the example below.

. . . .

We were each standing there with a welcome
drink in our hand, talking about the weather. For
the extroverts, it was clearly an easy game. For
me, it was something I had to perform. While the
extroverts seemed to derive energy from this easy
sociability, I became more and more tired, scouting
for someone I could have a deeper conversation
with. I knew that that was what I needed in order to
get my energy back.

Lars, age 47

. . . .

When I am waiting, for example at a bus stop, I prefer
to remain with my own thoughts instead of conversing
with those around me. But if it makes sense for me, I
can fall into conversation – even with people I do not
know. For quite a while, I have been preoccupied with
selling my books to foreign publishers. This made me
very interested in other countries and their cultures.
When I hear a foreign accent, I immediately set off in
that direction – whether at a course, a badminton club,
or a bus stop. In those situations, I do not think at all
about whether it sounds awkward when I try to make
contact. I get the introductory small talk over with as
soon as possible; and, on a few occasions, it actually
turned out that the person helped me find a publisher
or translated an email into that person's language. In
addition, many pleasant and inspiring experiences
came out of it. So, I can warmly recommend making
use of a different strategy than the one you feel safest
with. There is actually not much an extrovert can do

that an introvert cannot also do. It just requires more strength, and you become tired more quickly when, as an introvert, you act in an extroverted fashion.

Introverts can have a hard time being the centre of attention. If I have to participate in a round of introductions, my heart often palpitates, and I botch what I say about myself. But, with time, I have come to enjoy giving lectures even to groups over 100 people. Of course, I get a little nervous at the start; but once I have had enough time to warm up to the situation, I enjoy having the space to talk about things with which I am deeply engaged. However, I could not do it unprepared. My thorough preparation makes me secure in the situation. I would rather not do it several times a day. Before the lecture, I need to rest alone; and, afterwards, I am so tired that I do not have the energy to be outgoing any more that day.

If you are an introvert, you are probably not especially attracted to the idea of getting up and speaking in front of a lot of people. But practice makes perfect. If you really want to and keep at it, you will reach a point where the situation feels familiar and secure.

If you are an introvert, you also need a longer time to process impressions than extroverts do. Perhaps others have said to you that you think too much about things or should take life less seriously. This is explained in the example below.

. . . .

When I have experienced something new, I like to walk by myself and process the impressions. I want to understand the connection between the experiences I already have and the new ones I've just had. It is as if I have a huge, internal map of the world and myself. Every time I've had a new experience that rocks my view of myself or the world, I feel like my inner map (with all its layers) comes into my consciousness, and it fills up my inner work desk for a time. During this period, I need to be alone. My friends sometimes get worried about me. They think I look gloomy when I am processing new impressions. But I just need peace and quiet to take some long walks in nature by myself. Then, everything falls into place in a new way, and I find that I have become wiser about the world and myself.

Simon, age 38

. . . .

Introverts can enjoy being alone and typically like nature, where they can roam in solitude or with someone who does not talk too much. It can quickly become stressful for them if they have to relate to the person or persons they are together with all the time. This is illustrated in the example below.

. . . .

I like being with others in a way that does not disturb my inner life too much. I love when my boyfriend and I are sitting at each end of the sofa with a book or a tablet, each with a cup of coffee on our own little coffee tables. I enjoy feeling the warmth of his leg and find it nice to be with him and, at the same time, be able to plunge into what I'm absorbed in at that moment.

Pernille, age 27

Introverts rarely speak just to say something. If you are an introvert, you would probably rather not be with others just to have someone to talk to as a rule. There should, preferably, be a deeper intimacy or a common interest, as shown in the example below.

In most contexts, I am typically quiet and withdrawn and do not say very much. But if I happen to be talking about something that interests me, I can go on for a long time. I like being in situations in which people share knowledge about a subject that interests me. If the topic is interesting enough, I can't keep myself from sharing what I know or asking questions, and have a hard time stopping again.

Jesper, age 33

If you are an introvert, you are probably not crazy about group work and would rather work independently. Basketball and football, where you have to be part of a team, are probably not the branches of sport you are most attracted to. Badminton, yoga, athletics, or other forms of sport that you pursue either alone or with only a few others do not demand nearly so much of you.

Introverts often move around quietly and calmly without huge gestures and without attracting much attention. If you are an introvert, you have probably had the experience of being overlooked. Many introverts talk about incidents in which what they have said was ignored but, later, when someone else said exactly the same thing – only in a louder voice and with greater self-confidence – it won applause. If you find that what you said has not been taken seriously, it is not necessarily because it was not relevant, wise, or correct. It is just a part of our culture that we listen most to extroverts.

I know this from myself. When I listen to a well-spoken, self-confident person, I momentarily forget everything I know and am capable of. Only when I get home on my own and ponder what that well-spoken person really had on his or her mind do I realise that the actual content of what this person said only contained a repetition of what I had heard before in different contexts, while what I myself never got out was far more original and well-conceived. Perhaps you have found that you did not share your thoughts because you were unsure about whether what you had on your mind was sufficiently wise and relevant. At any rate, it is an experience I have heard many introverts talk about.

In the workplace, introverts like calm surroundings. Extroverts can more easily see the advantages of open-plan offices, where there is freer access to social contact. For introverts, the phone conversations of others can be a source of distraction and great irritation. They achieve their best results when they can work undisturbed in a quiet environment, where they can disappear into deep concentration or a state of 'flow'.

Whereas extroverts most often have their 'Aha!' experiences while they are talking, introverts need to be alone so they can think more deeply about what they have experienced – or talked to others about. Every now and then, I am actually impressed by how deeply extroverts are actually able to delve into a subject while they are talking. I am often inspired to new insights during conversations but need to be alone in order to draw my final conclusions.

Introverts do not have as many friends as extroverts do. But the friends they have they cultivate conscientiously. Whereas extroverts typically throw parties for their friends, introverts may be more inclined to offer concern when they sense there might be a need for it, like Sofie in the example below.

> If I haven't heard from my friend in a long time, I get worried. So, I text her and ask whether everything is all right with her. If I sense from her answer that she is not exactly doing great, I ask whether there is something I can help with.
>
> *Sofie, age 31*

When you are trying to assess whether a person is an introvert or extrovert, you would typically ask the following question today: 'Are you energised most from being alone or from being in the company of others?' That is to say, when you feel tired, do you seek company or would you rather be alone? If your predominant need is to be alone when you are tired, you are probably an introvert. But even the most introverted people need company now and again – and they, too, will find that company provides energy if they have been alone for a long time.

C.G. Jung, the first person to describe these two personality types, distinguished them in a different way. According to him, what characterises extroverts is primarily their interest in the external, material world, in people and activities. Introverts, on the other hand, are more interested in experiences in their own inner world of thoughts, dreams, desires, and fantasies – or that of other people. Instead of being absorbed by the external world for its own sake, introverts are more interested in feeling what the external world does to them and finding meaning in what takes place.

If C.G. Jung were to ask a question that separated introverts from extroverts, it would sound like this in contemporary language: 'Do you make your decisions primarily on the basis of the experiences of others or objective information you find outside yourself – or is your most important measure what is experienced as good or true inside?'

For introverts, the most important thing is that a given decision seems to them to be correct. This does not mean that they do not seek relevant information outside themselves, but the final word goes to their own personal experience of what seems good to do. This is illustrated in the example below.

> When I make a decision, of course I get the necessary information. But then I need peace and quiet. In fact, I prefer to sleep at least two nights on all major decisions and have plenty of time, for example, to walk alone in nature. In the best-case scenario, I experience at some point a clear inner sense of which way I should go.
>
> *Preben, age 45*

Many introverts are also very sensitive. But not all. This is obvious from the very fact that 30–50 per cent of the population are presumed to be introverted, while only 15–20 per cent are presumed to be highly sensitive.

The highly sensitive trait

It was more than 20 years ago that the American psychologist and researcher Elaine Aron described the highly sensitive character trait. Many books have been written on the subject since then. There is great interest in it.

If you are highly sensitive, you have probably been able to recognise yourself in most of my description of the introverted personality type. Highly sensitive people also think a lot about life and themselves. They need time alone. They need to search their inner feelings or intuition when they make decisions.

They prefer to be well-prepared for most of their activities and do not care for conflict.

Often, high sensitivity is connected to being extra 'five-sense' sensitive, that is, very susceptible to the impressions that come through the senses. There are both upsides and downsides to this. For example, you will be bothered more easily than others by sounds, smells, light, cold, or warmth. But you will also feel positive sense impressions more strongly – for example, nice scents, a beautiful view, a loving caress, or a wonderful piece of music – and this can be both moving and very joyful.

We share 'five-sense' sensitivity with many other types of people. People with autism, for example, can be very 'five-sense' sensitive. The same holds true for people with post-traumatic stress disorder (PTSD). You can also become extra 'five-sense' sensitive, for example from a brain concussion, from too little sleep, or from having succumbed to stress.

Beyond being extra 'five-sense' sensitive, highly sensitive people are typically creative, conscientious, and empathic.

IF YOU ARE HIGHLY SENSITIVE, YOU WILL PROBABLY
ANSWER NO TO MOST OF THE STATEMENTS BELOW

~ I think our annual Christmas party at work should last at least 12 hours.

~ I love exciting adventure tours, where you don't know in advance what is going to happen.

~ I eat pretty much anything and am neither fussy nor picky.

~ I sleep heavily and well at night and am not disturbed by light or sound.

~ I think a brisk fight is refreshing.

~ I thrive in environments where there are a lot of activities at once.

ON THE OTHER HAND, YOU WILL PROBABLY ANSWER YES TO MOST OF THE FOLLOWING STATEMENTS

~ When I have seen or heard something about the suffering of other people, it can affect my mood for a long time.

~ I suffer from a bad conscience easily.

~ I am very creative or have a lively imagination.

~ I am often disturbed by smells or sounds that most other people do not seem to be bothered by.

~ If I am too cold or too hot, I cannot ignore it but have to change the temperature or go somewhere else.

~ I do not care for conflict.

At the conclusion of the book, you can find a comprehensive self-test that can give you a number for how sensitive you are.

Highly sensitive people can be very different. For example, I am not particularly bothered by strong light, but sounds I do not like can drive me crazy. Some highly sensitive people do not think of themselves as creative. And it is not necessarily the case that they always are. You can be highly sensitive without being able to see all the characteristics of being a highly sensitive person in yourself. But it can also be the case that highly sensitive people actually are creative but just have not had the opportunity to cultivate their creativity. Many highly sensitive people struggle so hard to live up to what other people can do or endure that they are more or less over-stimulated most of the time. If you are to get in touch with your creative side, it requires time and patience to dig deeper.

In order to understand high sensitivity in depth, you must become familiar with the recognised American researcher Jerome Kagan's discoveries about the high-reactive temperament. Elaine Aron bases a large part of her research on Kagan's results. For example, when she writes that highly sensitive children are more conscientious and thrive better than average children under normal and calm circumstances, she refers to research that has been done on the behaviour of high-reactive children. She believes that these children are actually highly sensitive.

The high-reactive temperament

Jerome Kagan studies hereditary as opposed to environmental influences. In the beginning, he was convinced that environmental influences meant far more than heredity when it came to the development of different temperaments. However, he was forced to admit along the way that heredity had a great deal of significance.

In 1989, Kagan examined 500 four-month-old babies, whom he introduced to a variety of new impressions – for example, strange smells, a colourful mobile they had not seen before, strange voices, and other unknown sounds such as a popping balloon. Approximately every fifth child was upset by the strange impressions. They became uneasy, screamed, and gesticulated with their arms. Four out of five children remained calm.

Kagan examined many of the children again when they were 2, 4, 7, and 11 years old – and it turned out that there was a dominant tendency for the children who had been, in the first instance, uneasy when they were subjected to new impressions to continue to distinguish themselves. At first, Kagan called these children 'inhibited' because they were more reticent and cautious than the others. Later, he gave them the designation 'high-reactive'. This term describes a powerful internal reaction that is reflected in uneasy behaviour in infants. When the children grew older, their internal reaction could not necessarily be seen. What could be observed from the outside was that they were typically quiet, reticent, and reflective, and that they cried easily. Jerome Kagan's research is well-supported and recognised in wide scholarly circles.

As mentioned above, Elaine Aron believes that Kagan's high-reactive children and adults are actually highly sensitive. All highly sensitive people, according to Aron, are also high-reactive people.

I shall not go deeper here into what it means to be highly sensitive, since I have described it thoroughly in my first book, *Highly Sensitive People in an Insensitive World: How to Create a Happy Life*. However, I shall spend some time describing why many highly sensitive people view themselves as extroverts – and, in a certain sense, they are.

High sensitivity and introversion

You have probably noticed that there are many common features that introverts and highly sensitive people share. You may ask yourself whether there is any difference at all. There is no doubt that a number of introverts are not highly sensitive. As mentioned before, this is evident alone from the fact that 30–50 per cent of the population are presumed to be introverts, while only 15–20 per cent are presumed to be highly sensitive.

The question, then, is: are all highly sensitive people introverts? In the beginning, that is what Elaine

Aron thought, and she clearly based her description of highly sensitive people on Jung's description of the introverted personality type. But later she amended her original take a bit. The answer to whether introversion and high sensitivity are the same is both yes and no. In order to understand differences and similarities between the two types, it is important to distinguish between what Jung called 'extroversion' and what Aron calls 'social extroverts'.

When Aron, who is a pioneer in describing high sensitivity, writes that 30 per cent of all highly sensitive people are extroverts, she means that they are exclusively what she calls 'social extroverts'; and this is something different from what Jung wrote about. Jung's extroverts dominate easily, are willing to take more risks, and seize the opportunity to speak quickly and without a great deal of reflection. Most highly sensitive people do not – not even people whom Aron describes as 'social extrovert, highly sensitive'.

Elaine Aron also writes in an article from 2006 (Aron 2006, p.15) that the only difference between Jung's introverted types and her 'highly sensitive, socially extroverted' people is that the latter like meeting strangers, thrive in groups, and have many friends. The highly sensitive people, whom she calls 'social extroverts', therefore have at least as much in common with Jung's introverts as they do with Jung's extroverts.

All highly sensitive people are introverts in the sense that they reflect deeply about life and themselves and listen to their inner feelings or intuition instead of only navigating by markers outside themselves. But 30 per cent of them are, at the same time, social extroverts, understood in the sense that they have many friends, prefer to be in groups, and like meeting strangers. According to Aron, these 30 per cent typically grow up feeling comfortable among people – for example, at a boarding school, in a commune, or with a flock of siblings. Therefore, it feels 'homey' and safe for them to be with a lot of people.

As mentioned before, Elaine Aron believes that Jerome Kagan's high-reactive types are actually highly sensitive; according to Aron, he has just given them a different name. Kagan calls attention in several places to the similarity between high-reactive young people and Jung's introverts. As he wrote in *The Long Shadow of Temperament*, 'Carl Jung's descriptions of the introvert and extrovert, written over 75 years ago, apply with uncanny accuracy to a proportion of our high- and low-reactive adolescents' (Kagan and Snidman 2004, p.218). Once again, it is clear here how great the similarities are between high sensitivity and introversion since they both have a close relationship to Kagan's high-reactive personality types.

Personally, I can easily recognise what characterises Kagan's high-reactive personality types in myself. I am easily frightened and do not throw myself into something new without much prior consideration.

Only after I had identified myself for many years as an introvert did I discover Aron's research on high sensitivity. Now I view myself both as an introvert and as highly sensitive.

Nature or nurture

Elaine Aron believes that high sensitivity is innate but that you can also acquire this character trait through trauma. According to Jung, people are born with a disposition to develop either an introverted or an extroverted personality type. But environment can also push people in a different direction, so that they develop into a different type than the one to which they are genetically disposed.

If, for example, you are born with a disposition toward extroversion but have been subjected to trauma or simply rough treatment in childhood, you may be afraid of other people and choose to live an introverted life to protect yourself. And if you were born with a disposition toward introversion but quickly discovered that your parents liked you better when you behaved as an extrovert, you may have adopted an extroverted style. However, it costs something to develop an inclination that is different from the one to which you are genetically disposed. As Jung writes in his book *Psychological Types*: 'As a rule, whenever such a falsification of type takes place as a result of parental influence, the individual becomes neurotic later, and can be cured only by developing the attitude consonant with his nature' (Jung 1976, p.332).

I am often asked how you can know whether your personality type is in agreement with your natural disposition or whether it is conditioned by the environment. The types come into existence through an interchange between genetic disposition and external influences, and it is impossible to know in an individual case how much is due to one or the other. If you have a sense that you are more introverted or extroverted through external influences than seems, deep down, natural to you, you can experiment by training yourself toward the opposite lifestyle and see whether it increases your sense of well-being.

You may be able to get an indication of how much is genetic and how much is environmentally conditioned in your case by looking at your family. If one or both of your parents are highly sensitive or introverted, your type is probably inherited for the most part. But if you are the only sensitive or introverted person in your family, it is likely that environment played a large role. Perhaps there were circumstances in your childhood that made it necessary for you to behave in a particular way. Or perhaps there were traumas – perhaps shocking experiences that you no longer remember – that have left you with an inclination toward introversion or an extra-sensitive nervous system.

Some people become introverted, highly sensitive, or overly responsible from a painful childhood. But not everyone does. Others become anti-social, criminal, or violent from the same background. Those who are born with highly sensitive or even just born with a genetic disposition to be sensitive, and who also experience a lack of care early in life, may become overly adapted and so sensitive that they sense and align themselves with others to such an extent that they almost do not feel their own needs when others are present.

If you think that your sensitivity or introversion is predominantly due to your upbringing, you probably wonder whether it can be 'trained away or treated' in whole or in part. If you go to therapy and process your painful childhood, you may find that you are less anxious, and that shame about yourself is reduced. The increased insight you get from treatment will, among other things, make you more robust to the criticism of others and more capable of standing up for yourself and your needs. Perhaps you will also become more extroverted. But the increased sensitivity, wisdom, and ability to empathise with the sufferings of others that your circumstances have given you will not disappear.

Whatever the cause of your introversion or sensitivity may be, I hope the advice and tips in the next chapters will make your life easier and more meaningful.

Chapter 2

Screen Yourself from Too Many Impressions

Extroverts thrive and deliver their best work results when they are in stimulating surroundings. For example, they like listening to loud music while they work more than introverts do. Introverts deliver their best work results when there is peace and quiet surrounding them.

It can be very unpleasant to be in surroundings in which more is going on than you can handle. Perhaps you have had experiences that resemble Kasper's in the example below.

• • • • • • • • • • • •

We had already had a lot of information about the reorganisation that was going to take place at work when my boss said that there was an extra point under 'any other business' on which we also had to take a position. I just wanted to scream, 'No, no, I don't want to hear any more' – and run out of the room. However, I remained politely seated – but was out of balance for several hours afterwards.

Kasper, age 42

Or like Maria in the next example.

When I am very over-stimulated, for example after a major shopping trip, it helps to write everything down that I've experienced, to tell it to a good listener, or just to have peace and quiet around me for a bit, so I can quietly and calmly process the impressions. Until that is done, I am not entirely myself and can barely communicate. If I still have to be sociable in that situation, there is a huge risk I'll say something awkward.

Maria, age 27

It is important for everyone to know the level of stimulation that provides them with the greatest well-being. For introverts and sensitive people, the optimal level is typically considerably lower than it is for extroverts. But be aware that it can also be too low even if you are sensitive or introverted. It is not a matter of avoiding stimulation but of finding the level that is optimal for you.

The great challenge in having a lower threshold than most people for how much stimulation feels pleasant is to protect yourself against too many impressions. The following pages provide some advice on how to do this.

Create a breathing space for processing your thoughts

Each day, most of us receive a huge quantity of information and stimuli from our surroundings and from online communication. It is important every so often for us to stop the stream of information and give ourselves time and space to sort out these impressions. Here is a little exercise that can help:

Sit comfortably in a chair or on a meditation cushion. Perhaps keep a notebook at hand. Make sure your back is straight and your head is in line with your spine. Shake your shoulders a little to release tension.

Set a stopwatch for 5, 10, 15, or 20 minutes. I use the 'Insight Timer' app. It offers guided meditations but can also be used as a stopwatch. It can be downloaded free of charge onto your phone and provides a pleasant little 'pling' sound when time is up. When you are sitting comfortably and have set the stopwatch, close your eyes and take a few deep breaths, exhaling with a deep sigh. You can strengthen the experience by lifting your arms over your head as you breathe in and letting them fall as you breathe out. Then, let your respiration find its natural rhythm while you pay attention to it. Notice how it makes your body move. Focus on the body's extremities: hands, feet, and face. Notice the sensations that arise in those places where you direct your attention.

Up to this point, it resembles a mindfulness exercise. Here is the new twist: if a thought that pops up is superficial, let it go and turn your attention back to your breathing and your body's external poles. But if the thought that occurs to you has to do with a decision you need to take or an experience you have had recently that you have not yet quite come to terms with, then give it time. Let it unfold on your inner screen. Perhaps you can reach a decision or a greater understanding of the experience that has appeared in your thoughts.

It is important that you also take little breaks in your thinking along the way and focus on your body and breathing. If you use the 'Insight Timer' app as a stopwatch, you can have it remind you to stop when it makes a sound at various intervals along the way. When you turn back to your thoughts after a little break (during which you focus on your breathing), you can better assess whether they are fruitful or pointless musings.

If, during the exercise, you have thoughts that regularly appear and run in circles without getting anywhere, write them down and decide whom you should talk to about them. Then let them go and turn your focus back to your body and breathing.

You may have found that the art of paying attention to your thoughts and looking at them from the outside is not as easy as it sounds. But it is something you can become better at, the more you practise.

You can do the exercise, for example, when you are waiting for something. It is much better than checking your emails or being on social media. It provides you with an opportunity to elaborate on selected ideas, prepare yourself for decisions, or just give your senses a break from external impressions.

I do this little exercise almost daily and find that it perks me up.

Cut down on your news intake

You may think you have a duty to keep up with what is happening in the world. If you watch or listen to the news often, you may have experienced a feeling of dependency on it, that you check on it almost compulsively.

The media have a predilection for conflict. So, if you watch or listen to the news too much, you can easily – more or less, consciously – get the mistaken impression that there is far more violence than love in the world. This view can give rise to stress, insecurity, and bad moods.

It does no one any good for you to use your energy taking a position on all the problems of the world every day since you cannot do much about it anyway. If you have spent time recharging and digesting impressions, and have gained new energy and a somewhat blank slate, it is too bad to ruin everything, for example with brutal pictures of suffering people that will probably fill you with concern, sorrow, and (perhaps) a bad conscience because you are not doing anything about it.

How deeply people absorb images can vary. If you are the sort of person who may be affected for several days, I would recommend that you come up with a plan to limit your intake of news.

When I really have to concentrate on a project, I do not watch, listen to, or read any news. At regular intervals, however, I ask someone whether he or she might give me a censored résumé of what is happening in the world at that moment. Otherwise, I read about the news on the Internet – but never in the morning, when I am at my most vulnerable, nor last thing in the evening when it might get mixed up in my dreams. I prefer to get my news once, some time during the afternoon.

On the other hand, every so often I like to see a thorough documentary about a conflict in the world or to listen to knowledgeable people discuss it on serious television programmes. Here, I find that increased knowledge about a problem can sometimes have a dampening effect on my otherwise easily aroused catastrophic thinking.

Do not be bullied by your phone

A phone call can be very disturbing, for example if you are deep inside a creative process. Especially if the person who is calling wants you to take a position on something or other or expects you to react with a particular feeling – such as pleasure at the call or an invitation.

Many introverts or highly sensitive people like to have their phone set on silent. They can check it later when they need a break anyway from whatever they are occupied with. Then, they can write an email or text back to ask what it is about before they decide whether to return the call.

Screen yourself from too much social contact

Ear plugs, ear buds, and dark sunglasses can help protect you. If you work in an open office, it may be possible to put up screens.

Introverts can concentrate best if no one can see their face while they are working – and, particularly, if they can be sure that a person cannot suddenly be standing right in front to them, without warning, staring them in the face. They are capable of concentrating so deeply that their face relaxes into folds that can make them look depressed. An extrovert who catches sight of a deeply concentrated introvert might easily become frightened or worried.

I experience this myself when I go for walks in the summer in bare feet. Slowly, I saunter along, gathering up all my experiences: the warm summer wind against my skin, the warm asphalt or earth beneath my feet, birdsong, and smells – dog roses, especially, can exhilarate me. At the same time, I am often absorbed by thoughts, ideas, or problems I need to solve. It is not rare that somebody stops me and asks whether something is wrong, whether they can help with anything. It is nice of them but terribly disturbing. I am ripped from an enjoyable reverie or a productive train of thought and have to put on my social mask. It takes a long time for me to return to my almost meditative enjoyment.

If you are somewhere others can see your face or there is a risk that someone will suddenly turn up in front of you, you probably use energy to avoid letting your face relax into folds that can frighten some random observer. Once those around you have learned not to disturb you unexpectedly, you will have more energy available to concentrate on what you are working on.

It can be difficult to reject social contact without feeling impolite. Many sensitive people and introverts accept much more social contact in the workplace and privately than they care for.

The unwritten rules for when and how we can contact each other favour extroverted personality types to a high degree. Put simply, they go like this:

~ You may not interrupt a person who is speaking.

~ Whoever is the quickest to formulate their thoughts and keeps talking the longest without needing a break may dominate.

~ It is always valuable to start a conversation. If a person is silent, you can say, for example, 'Now, listen to this story,' and then proceed to tell it.

~ You may not end a conversation while someone is speaking. You have to wait for the person to finish speaking and, to be certain, there should be a small break after the last word is said before you suggest going your way.

Unwritten rules often need to be challenged. I have created an alternative set of rules. You can read these alternative rules on the placard on the next page.

♥

SPEAK OR BE SILENT
☞ guide to good manners

~ YOU MAY NOT INTERRUPT A SILENCE unless you have something important to say. And even though it may be important, you may not begin to speak before the listener has given you the green light.

~ If you have spoken without interruption for more than a minute, you must take a break. TAKE A DEEP BREATH, and think about how relevant what you are saying is for the person(s) to whom you are speaking. If no one encourages you to continue, you should keep quiet and ALLOW OTHERS A CHANCE to say what is on their mind.

~ You may NOT interrupt people who are lost in their own thoughts.

~ If someone asks whether he or she may say something to you, you must give yourself time to determine whether YOU WANT TO LISTEN to this person and whether the time is right. If not, you may just shake your head. You do not need to apologise or explain.

The idea is not for these new rules to be taken literally. They probably would not work in practice. The idea is to raise questions about the unwritten rules we follow in advance, to encourage anarchism in relation to outdated conventions, and to point out that there can be many other ways to be together with others.

You can download the placard with the new rules from http://highlysensitive-hsp.com/speak-silent. It can be used to start a conversation about the way we come into contact with each other.

How you can screen yourself in a group context

Sometimes we find ourselves in situations that are difficult to get out of. When I was a parish pastor, I lived and worked in the same place, and this had the great advantage that work was not far from a calm space where I could take a break. I liked most of my tasks as a parish pastor, but there was a single, recurring, annual event that filled me in advance with worried thoughts and, subsequently, left me completely exhausted for several days. That was the annual late summer excursion when the church council and the congregation went somewhere for the whole day by bus.

As a member of the church council, I had some influence on where we would go, and I struggled to convince the others that we should choose a place that was not too far away. I never really succeeded, since a number of the others were adventurous and thought that the farther away something was, the more interesting it would be. At that time, I did not realise exactly why the excursion was so distressing for me and I could not clearly express myself.

Today, I can understand my reaction better. Beyond the fact that I suffered slightly from car sickness, it is very difficult to find peace and take a break on your own when you are a pastor with her flock on an outing. I was always afraid that I might break down crying in the bus from exhaustion. However, I was always able to keep myself together until I reached the door of the parsonage.

It was fortunate for me that it was only on one day a year that I was really challenged. In other workplaces, people have to endure staff weekends, Christmas parties that last half a day or more, team-building courses, and other activities that most extroverts love but which can fill introverts with stress and discomfort.

When you are over-stimulated, it is unpleasant to be in a social context and painful to have to receive even more information. If you are one-on-one, you can withdraw or ask for a break. But if you are in a group of people who seem to be enjoying themselves at a lecture, for example, you cannot just ask the speaker to be quiet.

When I held a talk in Greenland in 2015, the staff member at Nuuk Library who had arranged the lecture warned me in advance that if a Greenlander did not think the lecture was saying anything to him or her, the person would just get up and leave. And, right enough, there were a few who left the library before I was finished. I actually think it is a good custom and nice to know that those who remained were not just sitting there because they thought it was too awkward to leave.

In Denmark, we are often so polite that we remain seated much longer than we would like. For most people, it is not such a big problem; but for sensitive or introverted people, it can sometimes be extremely painful if they are unable to close their ears or escape listening to more.

I have adopted Greenland's custom. I tiptoe out as discreetly as possible if I no longer feel it is pleasant or meaningful to stay. If you can only take information in limited quantities, it is a shame if you have to use your limited listening capacity on something that neither feels nice nor makes sense to you.

If, for some reason, I do not leave the room, I use another method to shut out the information. I keep in my bag small, almost invisible ear buds. I take them out discreetly and hide the cords in my hair or a scarf. Then, I let some wonderful music drown out the speech that is going on. I can still have quite a good time being in a group of people – just on my own terms. I avoid disturbing others and myself by getting up and leaving – and I can choose to be partially there. Every so often, I turn down the music and listen to the stream of words. Then, I turn it up again if what is being said is not sufficiently relevant to me.

What to do if you cannot prevent unpleasant over-stimulation

Sometimes, it is not possible to screen yourself sufficiently. Time and again, introverts or highly sensitive people find that they become so stressed from too many activities or impressions that it can be a long time before they feel like they are themselves again.

Perhaps you have been over-stimulated to such a degree that you were no longer able to be creative and, therefore, could do nothing but throw yourself in front of the television, surf the Internet, or go to bed. None of these things helps against over-stimulation. There is a need for calm if impressions are to fall into place in your *waking* consciousness. However, you do not need to be completely quiet. It is a question of finding activities in which you do not need to relate to new impressions.

This can vary from person to person. A good thing to do when you are over-stimulated, I would suggest, is to make your own list and save it in your phone, so that it is easily accessible. Below are some suggestions.

ACTIVITIES THAT MAKE SENSE TO ENGAGE
IN BUT ARE NOT STIMULATING

~ All forms of routine tasks: cleaning, peeling vegetables, ironing, mowing the lawn, weeding the garden, etc.

~ Knitting.

~ Baking.

~ Running.

~ Doing yoga or Pilates.

~ Moving around in the room to music. Let your body decide your movements.

~ Taking a bath or a footbath.

EXPRESS YOURSELF

~ Tell your experiences to someone who is a good listener.

~ Write in your diary.

~ Do something creative: paint, make music, or do something similar.

Beyond writing in my diary, it works particularly well for me to spend half a day cooking – not new dishes but dishes I can make routinely. I enjoy listening to my favourite music while I peel vegetables, cut them up, and stir the pan. When I am done, I fill my freezer with dishes in small portions – easy to take out after a stressful day. In the meantime, I have sorted out impressions and, perhaps, thought things through and made the necessary decisions.

Stimulation, however, can also come from the inside. So, keep an eye on what your thoughts are, circling around. More on that in the next chapter.

Chapter 3

LIMIT YOUR CATASTROPHIC THINKING

When you are a sensitive soul, it can be a good thing to be prepared for the worst and the best. If you are prepared, the risk of being overwhelmed is less. Many highly sensitive or introverted people are careful to make themselves emotionally and mentally prepared for what is going to happen. If you have already imagined various scenarios and made a plan A and a plan B for what you will do, it can give you security and peace of mind and lessen the risk that you will be over-stimulated in the situation.

However, some highly sensitive or introverted people have such a lively and vivid imagination that their ideas often circle around catastrophes such as, 'What if there is a war in my country?' or 'What if a nuclear war breaks out?' or 'What if there is some unexpected natural disaster because of climate change?' or 'What if I – or one of my loved ones – get a life-threatening or crippling disease or meet with a serious traffic accident?' It is not a problem if your thoughts are preoccupied every now and then with possible future misfortunes. Indeed, these thoughts may arouse a feeling of gratitude that you have been spared them up to now. But if you are regularly caught up with making yourself emotionally ready for catastrophes and accidents, it may give you a chronic feeling of unease.

If one of these catastrophes really were to happen, it would not help very much to have spent time putting together a plan B, because the reality would undoubtedly be quite different from what you had imagined and planned for in advance. When thoughts of catastrophe arise, therefore, I would suggest that you stop them and say to yourself, 'If the worst happens, I'll deal with it.' In all probability, something good will come from misfortune. Perhaps, in a given case, you will fight side by side with people who will become friends for life.

The worst thing about imagining catastrophes is that you can easily see the images in your inner eye, but you cannot act upon them. Should they happen, you can act, and then it is rarely as bad as you had imagined beforehand.

You may think that you will fare more poorly than others because you are an introvert or highly sensitive person. The truth is probably the opposite. Viktor Frankl was a professor in neurology and psychiatry in Vienna. He was Jewish and survived three years in the concentration camp of Auschwitz. He believed that those who fared best under these catastrophic conditions were those who were good at finding meaning in suffering – for example, by helping others – and that is what introverts and highly sensitive people are often especially good at. So do not believe your chances are poorer if a great catastrophe should take place. Perhaps, to the contrary, you will, in the midst of disaster, be creative in a new way, find deeper meaning for your life, and forge loving bonds with those you are with.

The same holds true about the end of life, and it is true of death. It is good to be conscious of the fact that you will one day be gone, to be prepared, and to take some precautions. Perhaps you have saved for retirement, found a place to live without too many stairs, done what you can to live healthily, and stayed in shape. However, there are limits to how much it is good for you to think about death and decay. If you often think about how you are getting more and more wrinkles, are becoming less sexually attractive, and may ultimately succumb to a series of illnesses, it will have an effect on the happiness you get from life.

Create a pleasant image of the future

Do not let images of illness and decay fill your inner screen in your daily life. Create some positive images as a counterweight. Most older people do not care so much about how they appear in the eyes of others. They become more authentic and have greater courage to reveal themselves and to be honest and stand up for themselves. This increased courage provides an opportunity for deeper and more meaningful contact even with people they do not know so well.

Imagine how much fun your life could be if you let go of the dream of being perfect. Gradually, fewer demands would be placed on you. Even if, in the worst-case scenario, you spend your final days sick and feeble in a hospital or nursing home, there is still hope. It is not too late to experience loving encounters with others – indeed, sometimes, it is actually easier when death has come closer, and the masks fall away.

You can prepare yourself for your death by regularly asking yourself throughout your life, 'What would I like to be remembered for when I am dead?' or 'What would I like to look back on when I say goodbye to life?' Then, you will know how to prioritise your life.

What happens in or after death, we do not know with certainty. So, we may as well create some positive conceptions. You may even be inspired by the near-death experiences of others. There is an entire literature in which people who have been dead for a few minutes talk about their experiences. Most people talk about light, love, and clarity.

There is no reason to live with an image of death as a black hole of nothingness. In my eyes, it is entirely too unimaginative. If your conception of death casts a stressful pallor over your life, I would suggest that you use your imagination and your creative abilities to imagine something nicer and more beautiful for yourself.

Chapter 4

FIND JOY AND MEANING

Highly sensitive and introverted people sometimes lack energy. Energy and joy are pretty much the same thing. Great joys that come as a surprise, however, can over-stimulate and exhaust at first; but, over the longer term, they will provide far more energy than they take. As a rule, you can say that, if you experience something joyful, you get more energy.

There are two forms of joy. One we can call enjoyment, the other satisfaction. Enjoyment, for example, may be listening to a beautiful piece of music, eating your favourite meal, smelling the summer scents, or exchanging a kiss. Satisfaction is when you do something that gives joy to others or yourself in the long run. For example, when you have completed a creative project, repaired someone else's computer, or listened to someone else's problems and felt their relief. You typically remember satisfying experiences like this longer than experiences you enjoy. On the other hand, they require as a starting point that you have a surplus of energy to work with. It is important that you create for yourself a life in which there is room for both forms of joy.

Choose the right job

It often takes a bit longer to find the right job when you are an introvert or highly sensitive person. Sometimes, we have to try a number of different things before we find the right fit.

One client relates his experience in the example below.

• • • • • • • • • • • • •

I had an administrative job that I was happy with in many ways. But I worked in an office with two very talkative colleagues. I tried to hold out but became more and more irritated. After having tried to talk with them and explain that I needed peace and quiet, I was just met with, 'We all have to be here.' I couldn't see any other possibility except to quit, which I did.

Henrik, age 32

• • • • • • • • • • • • •

Others leave their job due to too much stress, draughts, or just a bad atmosphere. Sensitive people are not good at ignoring something that gives them discomfort – and they must sometimes opt for the last resort: to leave their job.

If you are an introvert or sensitive person, it is especially important for your occupation to have meaning for you personally.

Many choose a career that provides care for others. Typically, ever since they were children, they have been concerned with how the people around them are thriving. It provides a great deal of meaning for them to help ease the pain of others; and, therefore, they wind up contributing more than they can tolerate in the long run. Many highly sensitive people in the caring professions go down with stress. Those who are content to work in the caring professions part-time, however, talk about the joy and satisfaction they have in the job.

Others choose a routine job such as warehouse operator, cleaning or administrative assistant, mailperson, or the like. This has the great advantage that they are not over-stimulated at work. To the contrary, they can often process the impressions they have received outside work time while they are at work, so they are ready for new impressions when they come home.

Introverts and sensitive people also prefer self-employment. Here, their imagination and the wealth of their ideas can really unfold. They can make sure their workplace has the right level of noise, and the temperature that suits them best. They can control their work schedule to a large extent too. If they do not have obligations as a provider, they can often live on very little. It is not a high standard of living or status or plenty of material goods that makes a big difference to quality of life in highly sensitive or introverted people. Working independently, they can be content to earn the money they need – and then enjoy taking time off and doing other things the rest of the time. However, it can be a challenge to live with the economic uncertainty that often accompanies the life of a self-employed worker.

If you do not need to earn a lot of money, there are many options. A highly sensitive person I met at one of my lectures told me that, after trying many different jobs without being satisfied, she had decided to study at the university at a ripe old age. Living on student grants was not a problem for her. She already wore second-hand clothes since she wanted to be environmentally friendly. The calm that exists at university, where you can really go into a subject in depth, was good for her.

Many introverts and highly sensitive people like being managers. There is a great freedom in that. They typically have their own office, where they can close the door to be alone sometimes. They can influence the workplace with their ideas and often become beloved bosses because they have a good sense of the well-being of their co-workers and are good listeners. However, it can be a challenge in the beginning since many introverts or highly sensitive people do not care much for talking in front of a lot of people. Yet, it is something they can get used to –

and when they have made it over that hurdle, a job in management can be very satisfying.

Working with your hands or in the outdoors can also be very joyful. When I have held lectures for sensitive people, I have often asked whether there is someone who would recommend their job to other highly sensitive people. Gardeners, organic farmers, and nature guides, for example, are happy to. Creative jobs are also popular. Many authors, painters, and musicians are introverted or highly sensitive.

What you prioritise in your free time should also be either fun or joyful, so it provides you with energy. Or, at a minimum, it should give you the experience of doing something good in the world, so others get joy from it, and you experience satisfaction and meaning in turn.

Go to parties – well-prepared

Introverts are typically not crazy about going to big parties. Some do it anyway, and there can be many reasons for this. Perhaps you want to avoid having a bad conscience. Perhaps you like the birthday boy and want to please him by turning up. Or, perhaps, you would actually like to establish or keep contact with some of the guests.

When you go to a party even though you are not enthusiastic about it, you can make it easier for yourself in one or more of the following ways:

~ Plant the seeds for a scenario in which you can go home early without a bad conscience. As soon as you accept the invitation, you can say, for example, 'I hope it's okay if I only stay a few hours'; and, if you have the courage to be honest, you can also add, 'It is hard for me to be sociable for too long – I'll enjoy it more if I only stay a short while.' You can also ask the host whether there is a room or adjoining locale you may use if you need a break.

~ Acquaint yourself with the principles of small talk and how you can shift to a deeper form of contact. I have written about this in my book *Highly Sensitive People in an Insensitive World: How to Create a Happy Life*. Greater knowledge about how you do this can make it a bit easier.

~ In addition, prepare yourself for whom you would like to talk to and about what. Think about what topics give you energy – and, perhaps, how you could bring the topic up.

~ If you want to be even more thorough in your preparation, you can, for example, write to selected people in advance: 'I'm looking forward to seeing you and hope we have a chance to discuss...' or 'I hope I get an opportunity to tell you about..., I would like to hear your opinion.'

Often, it is the case at parties that extroverts like to discuss things around a large dinner table while introverts would rather withdraw into the corner, or maybe into the garden, to conduct conversations one-on-one or in small groups about the topics they are interested in. If two of you have had contact in advance about this mutual desire, you can give each other a glance across the dinner table and go outside.

You can also arrange a party yourself that lives up to your own wishes for how social interactions best play out. State the starting and ending times on the invitation. It can be difficult to know in advance how long you would like to have guests, and it is better to set an endpoint a little too early rather than a little too late. You can probably persuade your guests to stay a little longer if it feels too early to stop the party. It is far more difficult to ask them to go home a little earlier.

There are many ways to enjoy social interaction. Perhaps meals are to be enjoyed in silence and introduced with a quick course on mindful eating, which has to do with eating very slowly and being conscious of every nuance in taste. Perhaps the meal should be eaten at small café tables, where people are put together according to their interests. Perhaps you want the body to be more prominent at the party and not simply parked on a chair all evening. You can invite people to dance, to a silent footbath, to massage their own or other people's feet, to take a hike, or play games in the garden. There are many ways you can hold a party without needing to sit around a large table, eating and drinking and becoming more and more boisterous as the party progresses until only the most extroverted have a chance to express themselves.

Community and being together give life value and can be enjoyed in many different ways.

There can be advantages in having easy access to social contact

Many people probably think that the right place for an introvert or highly sensitive person to live is out in the country, where there is nature and quiet. It can be a good solution for many. But there can be other advantages to living where there is easy access to being together with others. Otherwise, there might be too little social contact. If it is troublesome to arrange a social gathering in the sense that it requires a lot of planning, some introverts give up in advance. Perhaps from the fear that they will not have the desire or the reserves for it when the day comes, or that they will not have the energy to be around other people as long as they think they will need to be, out of politeness. You may have had the experience of feeling tired and lethargic from social under-stimulation.

When my children were small, we lived in a large commune for six years. We were 26 children and adults who lived together in a former school. In many ways, it was a challenge. But beyond the fact that it was very practical to be one of so many who could, in shifts, take care of the shopping and the cooking, it was good for me to have easy access to social contact. I did not need to plan in advance but could initiate something when the desire for sociability struck me. Sometimes, for example, I went to the big common kitchen and made pancakes. As a rule, even before I was finished, there would be a cosy gathering of housemates in the kitchen. If people did not come on their own, you could ring a bell. That was a signal that someone thought we should gather together for some reason or other. If, a half-hour later, I wanted to be alone again, it was not a problem. The others just continued the good time without me.

However, you do not need to move into a commune in order to have easy access to social community. If you live close to friends or in a city, there is easier access to others than if you have pitched your tent in the country.

The pros and cons of online communication

Written communication by email or through social media has many advantages when you are an introvert or highly sensitive person. You can easily find groups with common interests, for example on Facebook. Here, you can share experiences and help each other to learn about a topic you find interesting. Written communication also has the advantage that you can participate at your own tempo. If someone asks about something, you can go away from the screen, get a cup of tea, and take all the time you need to consider your answer.

There are also many advantages to being able to limit social contact to short intervals without needing to abandon your safe cave and go out into an environment that may be over-stimulating or simply irritate your senses. All in all, it may be tempting to spend far too much time in front of a screen.

Moving outside to get face-to-face contact can sometimes require us to pull ourselves together and abandon our comfort zone even though there is always a risk that it will be a frustrating or over-stimulating experience. For example, when I decide to participate in a course or an event, I know myself well enough to understand that it may be a fleeting pleasure. I love playing badminton and participate in several badminton teams. The first time I go to a new place, I come up with a plan B so that, if they are playing loud music or put me through a hard warm-up, I can quickly go home again. The same holds true when I go to a concert. If the music is too loud or the sound quality is poor or it is too cold, it will not be long before I am sitting in my easy chair in front of the fire. Usually, however, it winds up being fun, and I thank myself afterwards because I pulled myself together and went.

Those times I decide to stay home, it can be tempting to try to meet my need for company by exclusively engaging in online communication. A whole day in which my only communication takes place online or by telephone leaves me, however, with a feeling of emptiness and frustration.

I am convinced that most of us need to be together with other people – face-to-face, live, preferably every day. There is a need to be involved in communication in which there is eye contact and your entire body language is part of the conversation. This provides a different form of satisfaction than online communication or a telephone conversation does. So, even though there are many advantages to staying home, I would recommend that, for your own good, you seek out face-to-face interaction every day as far as possible. Your fatigue may well be due to a lack of precisely this. Remember, it is not a matter of avoiding stimulation. It has to do with finding the right level and the right quality of stimulation to which you expose yourself.

Enjoy the company of both extroverts and introverts

With introverts, being together is often very simple. You can enjoy discussing a topic in depth together or just enjoy each other's company without many words. Highly sensitive or introverted people who gather in groups only for them and on their terms typically speak about it afterwards in enthusiastic phrases. Yet, it can also be quiet and dull for a long period of time.

In their eagerness to please the other person and avoid conflict, they sometimes forget to challenge or oppose each other properly. Here, extroverts have a lot to offer. Difference can also provide good energy, and many extroverts are easy and uncomplicated to be with. Perhaps, for quite some time, you have considered inviting over an extroverted friend, and now the right day has come. So, it is nice that he or she probably accepts without needing to think very long about it.

Be aware that extroverts easily become insecure with a person who does not say very much, speaks slowly, or just enjoys sitting with his or her own thoughts, observing social life. I have often heard from extroverts, 'I get insecure when you say nothing and become very unsure where you are,' or 'I need to know what is going on inside your head.' I would like to accommodate this desire and have made it a habit when I am together with extroverts to say a little more than I myself have a need to. It may just consist of brief sentences such as, 'I don't feel like saying very much, but I enjoy being here,' or, 'If I seem a little absent every so often, it's because I'm absorbed in my own thoughts. It has nothing to do with you,' or, 'If I don't come to your party, it's not because I have anything against you. I'm actually impressed that you have the energy to invite us all over. I just need time and peace for myself.'

Making sure that your extroverted friends do not become insecure can pay off. You can also explain more about what it means to be an introvert or highly sensitive person, if they would like to hear about it. Many misunderstandings can be avoided if you are familiar with each other's personality type.

Over the course of time, many introverts and highly sensitive people have tried to be just as fresh, energetic, and sociable as extroverts. Being together can be very stressful if you try to be a particular way. It is important for you to stick to your own way of being even if you are with a different type of person. You probably enjoy the cheery energy that comes from being together with extroverted types. And they enjoy it when you listen to them. The more people take the risk to be different and contribute what they can, the better the contact is. If people try to be the same, it can easily become boring.

Contact becomes livelier when we dare to stand up for ourselves. It is perfectly okay to be an introvert or highly sensitive person and to act in ways that fit your type. This is also true when boundaries are to be set. You do not need to do it in a confrontational, extroverted fashion. But more about that in the next chapter.

Chapter 5

Deal with Conflicts and Boundaries in Your Own Way

Introverts and highly sensitive people typically do not care to set boundaries or become part of a conflict. Sometimes, we put off a confrontation again and again because the right time and the right means never seem to materialise. At other times, we become involved in disagreements, and it can cost us dearly in terms of energy.

If we still sometimes find ourselves in the middle of a power struggle, it may be, for example, because some of us are very sensitive about justice. Things need to be just – or we can react quite sternly. It is rare for us to shout or slam doors. The reaction is often an internal reaction in the first instance. We feel an internal agitation like Kagan's high-reactive children whom I described in Chapter 1. This internal agitation steals our peace of mind – and, sometimes, also our good night's sleep. It makes a huge dent in our ability to concentrate and in our stock of energy. Therefore, it is especially important to us not to engage in more battles than necessary.

How to back out of a power struggle – with dignity

It is good that some people quickly see that something is unjust and are, perhaps, even ready to fight for justice. At the same time, however, much energy can be saved by letting go of your right instead of going to war.

Once, I was outraged that I was charged a 7 euro late fee even though I knew for certain that I had paid on time. Later, I learned to let go of disputes over small amounts of money or anything else without significant value. It takes two to tango. It only takes one person to stop a fight. It may be that I will write a letter and call attention to a mistake, but if I sense that it will be a difficult struggle, I let it go.

You can back out with dignity if you speak your mind about what is going on. For example:

~ 'I do not agree with you, but I am not going to go to war over it.'

~ 'I disagree with the way you've calculated that, but I don't want to fight and I've transferred the money.'

> ~ 'I think you are breaking our agreement, but I don't want to waste any more energy discussing it. Go your way in peace.'

It is not weak to back out of a power struggle. It is wise and a sign of strength. There is so much else in life that provides much greater meaning to invest your thoughts and feeling in. With that said, we should still not put up with all forms of injustice and bad behaviour. Sometimes, someone has to say stop.

Should you confront the person directly?

Many of us have learned that, when you have to say no to someone or set boundaries for them, you should say it directly to the person, face-to-face. But if you are a sensitive person, this kind of direct confrontation can be so terrifying or unpleasant that you put it off and put it off and, ultimately, never get your boundaries marked.

Some sensitive or introverted people find an easier way to deal with negative encounters, such as Majbrit in the example below.

> As a rule, I send a text to the person in question in which I explain my thoughts and feelings. That takes the top off the emotions I'm afraid I might express since I find them childish and all too intense. Afterwards, I have a talk with the person, face-to-face. I don't know whether I'm handling it well since it is probably cowardly to send a text instead of dealing with them upfront.
>
> *Majbrit, age 46*

The advantages of writing instead of speaking directly are many. Introverted and highly sensitive people are typically most in touch with their inner feelings when they are alone and have plenty of time to consider their actions. Writing, they can very easily find the right formulation and, perhaps, also the courage to be entirely honest and true to themselves. I have never understood why it is supposed to be more correct to speak directly to someone instead of writing to them.

Myself, I would rather receive messages to which I react emotionally – for example, a rejection – in writing. Then, in peace and quiet, I can take a position with respect to the situation, cry about it if I need to, or find positive aspects to the new situation. It is difficult for me to process a piece of information that affects me emotionally at the same time as being in a social situation.

There are, however, also disadvantages to writing instead of meeting and talking about things. The risk that what was written can be misunderstood is great if you cannot hear the tone or see the facial expression.

On the phone, the risk of misunderstanding is a little less because the tone also contains information. Face-to-face, the chances for misunderstanding are the least. However, if you are very sensitive, a direct confrontation can be so overwhelming that your contact with yourself becomes poor. Therefore, you only discover what it was you really should have said after you get home – or, maybe, several days later. What you say instead in the situation may feel entirely wrong afterwards because you were too over-stimulated to feel and formulate something true and right and, therefore, just reeled off something to get out of the situation.

If the receiver is an extrovert, however, that person may find it devastating to receive a rejection or some other sad or disappointing news while he or she is alone. You can prevent this by ending your message with an offer to speak on the phone or to meet if the receiver needs that.

Phone calls also have advantages over a personal meeting when you need to set a boundary. If the conversation becomes unpleasant and you lose your thread or your contact with yourself and your message, you can more easily ask for a break and offer to call again, for example in half an hour. And if the other person begins to shout, you can hold the telephone away from your ear.

Manual for people who love a sensitive or introverted person

Perhaps you have found that irritation and anger can knock you off balance. If those closest to you realise how harshly aggression can affect you and provide you with a helping hand, it will be easier to deal with the necessary confrontations and find a solution to the conflicts that arise in every relationship.

I put together a questionnaire to which 45 highly sensitive people in Denmark responded regarding how they would prefer others to react to them when there is anger in a relationship. I was surprised how many different answers I got. But there were still some recurrent trends.

I have put these into a leaflet for people close to a sensitive or introverted person, which you can see on the next page. It may not be entirely suitable for you, but you may be able to use it as inspiration to create your own personal wish list for how you would like those around you to act when there is irritation or anger between you. You can print out the leaflet as a poster from my homepage: highlysensitive-hsp.com/sensitivity-anger.

The idea is not to create a set of commandments for your partner or whoever it might be with whom you have a relationship. You can give it to them as a wish list and use it as a starting point for a discussion about how you each function best when there is a disagreement or conflict hanging over you. Perhaps you can find a compromise with respect to how you will act toward each other in situations in which irritation or anger arises.

My questionnaire also revealed that many highly sensitive people are ashamed of worrying so much about conflicts.

When one of us is angry – how do you get the best out of me?

~ Don't shout, because then I become shocked and afraid and lose any ability to listen to what you are saying.

~ If you express yourself too violently, I will probably forgive you later, but I will be shaken to my core, and my nervous system will probably be affected and out of balance for several days. This will happen even though it ended with a reconciliation, and you may think it was good to clear the air.

~ Tell me quietly and calmly what it is that's making you angry and what you want me to do differently. Then, I will be extremely cooperative, and use all my empathy to try to understand you, and all my creativity and imagination to find a solution we both can live with.

~ When I am angry, you need to give me time. I need to find my peace of mind – and I may withdraw from you while I find it. You will certainly find out what is wrong, but I need a long time to think it through and formulate what I want to say.

~ Please stay calm while I tell you what it is. If you interrupt or react with anger, I will freeze up. And if I feel you are not listening, I won't be able to concentrate to finish. I will lose my thread of thought and my desire and energy to finish what I was saying.

~ Know that the situation feels dangerous to me – and I need your understanding.

It is entirely okay to worry about a conflict

Many introverted or highly sensitive people have been told that they need to stop worrying so much. Of course, it is a shame to spend so much energy worrying – especially when it sometimes turns out that the situation is not at all 'dangerous' and all that concern turns out to have been wasted.

For example, if you have imagined that your boss will be extremely displeased if you have done a task in your own way, you may have worried half the night or whole nights about it. If it proves, then, that she only has praise for you, you may regret having invested so many feelings and thoughts in worry. On the other hand, if it turns out that your presumption is correct and your boss criticises your work, your preparations may keep you from going entirely into shock and saying something you will later regret. Instead, you can respond to his criticism in a mature and well-considered way that benefits your interest in the firm in the long run.

If you are the one dissatisfied with your boss or, perhaps, with your partner or a colleague, imagining and speculating about things in advance can help you find a way to formulate what you want to say, so that problems will be solved in an orderly and undramatic way.

It is important for me to emphasise that thorough, advance considerations are part of having a sensitive nature, just as sensitive animals observe things for a

longer time before they act. It is a wise thing to watch out for yourself if you have a sensitive nervous system (hope you remember to speak lovingly to yourself) even if it turns out that these considerations were a waste of time.

If your speculations are completely out of proportion – so that they rob you of a good night's sleep, for example – even when it is simply a matter of a small disagreement, it is a good idea to get help. Find someone to talk to about it. Perhaps you know someone who is good to talk to about thoughts and feelings. Otherwise, you can talk to your doctor about it or seek out a professional psychotherapist or psychologist. It can be difficult to assess whether your speculations are out of proportion. I would think it is better to seek help one time too many than one time too few. It is a waste of energy to lug around a lot of problems that others could help you with if only they were allowed.

It is okay to calculate consequences in advance

A number of sensitive people do not like to think of themselves as using this strategy. It is presumably because they mix up 'making a calculation' with 'being calculating'. The latter I connect with trying to be manipulative and getting the most out of the situation or the relationship – to one's own advantage.

But when sensitive or introverted people try to calculate consequences in advance, as a rule it is because they would like to avoid situations that become unpleasant – not just for themselves but often just as much for the other person. Perhaps, in advance of an important conversation, you have conducted an internal dialogue such as the following: 'If he says this, I will say this..., then he will probably say this, and so I'll answer..., and if he is hurt, I will emphasise how much I appreciate his humour, for example, and how much I care about him.'

It may be a good thing to prepare before an important conversation. If many emotions come into play during a discussion, you may have experienced yourself slowing down and, sometimes, coming to a complete halt. Then, it can be a good thing to have prepared something in advance. Not everyone has the ability to calculate how a conversation will go. It requires empathy and imagination. Of course, it can be exaggerated and may affect your spontaneity in your contact with others. But it can also save yourself and others from unpleasant situations or, sometimes, just from boredom.

You are allowed to feel – without being able to explain

If something feels wrong, you do not need to wait to say anything until you yourself understand and can explain it. You do not always understand your

own reactions. If you express a feeling without knowing why you feel it, you may fear that you will be asked why and will come up short because you cannot explain it. As if you always need to be held accountable.

Explanations are not that important. Often, they are more or less made-up stories about why we feel the way we do. Without explanations, things go better most of the time. For example, you can introduce it this way: 'I don't myself understand why, but I feel this way...'

Much of what we feel inside is puzzling and inexplicable. It is just the way things are. To be open and curious about your own inner self and that of other people, talking about it without trying to explain it, is a path to good, satisfying contact.

A statement about your own inner self is stronger and clearer without explanations. Take, for example, the statement 'I love you.' This would be destroyed by an explanation such as, 'I love you because you are so wise.' In many instances, a statement such as 'This does not feel right to me' can stand alone perfectly well. You do not necessarily need to explain. You may also take the time you need to become aware of your feelings.

Give yourself time to respond

Many highly sensitive and introverted people have high standards for how they should behave. This holds true, for example, with respect to how quickly, politely, and honestly they should answer someone who asks them something. Bad experiences can arise because sometimes, by responding too quickly, they say something they later regret. Perhaps, you have said yes to an invitation without properly examining your feelings; and, when you get home, you can sense that you have neither the desire nor the energy to attend.

Fortunately, there is something else you can do other than respond quickly and politely. You can give yourself time to search your feelings about whether you even have a desire to respond. A counter-question can be clarifying and gain time. If someone asks, for example, 'What are you doing on Sunday?', you can, at one extreme, answer, 'I'm not telling' – and, at the other extreme, answer honestly and without hesitation. There is a third option: if you investigate the matter a little more closely – for example, by asking, 'Why do you want to know?' or, as my daughter might have said, 'What for?' – the other person may then say, 'Because I thought it would be nice to see each other.' Then, you can decide whether you want company or not.

The same strategy can also be used for personal questions, for example, 'Why don't you have any children?' You do not stand to account to anyone who asks. You can permit yourself to enquire back, 'Why do you want to know?' – or 'Perhaps I'll tell you another time.'

Even though you use strategies to slow the tempo and give yourself time, you will probably experience again and again that you still will not be able to get in touch with your feelings properly or find the right formulation.

Go back if you botch something

I am often asked whether I can provide strategies for reacting more quickly in emotionally charged situations. Unfortunately, it often characterises sensitivity or introversion to be slow and, sometimes, to freeze up when you encounter negativity or feel pressured. An example of this is given below.

A year and a half ago, my uncle said to me that I should stop taking myself so seriously and start getting a happier, more fun life. I was flabbergasted and changed the subject without commenting on it. But I was hurt, and, later, I didn't want to be near him, much less look him in the eyes. I can feel how my eyes automatically shift every time he looks in my direction. I am also angry at myself that I did not react at the time.

Karin, age 32

If you do not express yourself in a situation, you can always return to it later. Perhaps you may be met with, 'Why didn't you say anything before?' The answer to the question is probably that you were shocked or over-stimulated and, therefore, could only figure out what you wanted to say after you had got in touch with your feelings. And regardless of the cause, there is no law setting an expiration date on the right to say what you wanted to say.

If there is something that continues to bother you, you can easily come back two years later and say what you wanted to say. For example, 'What you said to me last Christmas, I don't agree, and I still get angry every time I think of it' or 'I'm sorry if I hurt you. Please forgive me.' Whether it is positive or negative, it can be good to get something said if you are still thinking about it. You are always permitted to come back when you are ready – whether weeks or months or years have gone by.

Highly sensitive and introverted people need time. We would like to be honest and, at the same time, take care of ourselves or those we are with. We are not good at repressing unpleasantness in a relationship in which something is amiss. On the contrary, we feel it clearly, and it bothers us. The same holds true of the frustration that arises when we follow another's path instead of our own.

Chapter 6

MAKE YOUR CHOICES FROM YOUR INNER CONVICTION

When I got glasses, my mother told me always to remember to look in the mirror before I left the house to see whether my glasses were dirty. I was a little puzzled by this and wondered why it was more important to see clearly when you were outside than when you were inside. Not until many years later did I understand why my mother had said what she did. She was always concerned with how she (and I) appeared. What the neighbours might think was an important yardstick. She based many of her decisions in life on what she believed looked best.

Going for what looks best rather than going for what you feel and believe inside is a trap we can easily fall into.

For some people, their self-image is so important that they often sacrifice even love. The way they are viewed by others can be an idol to which they sacrifice the most incredible things, as the example below illustrates.

. . . .

Lene gave up a man who loved her because he had a lower social status than she did. She found it embarrassing to marry below her. She was afraid others would think that there had to be something wrong with her since she could not find a husband who was her equal.

. . . .

In the worst-case scenario, that is the way many of life's choices may go. You choose clothes, for example, not necessarily for what increases your comfort and, maybe, not even for what you like, but for what you believe seems the best or most correct in the eyes of others.

Some even choose their jobs or free-time interests, not based on what they like or what seems to them to be meaningful, but on what they think others will respect them the most for.

Perhaps you are familiar with the phenomenon of not choosing something that seems best for you because you are afraid of others' judgement. Perhaps, for example, you like to travel alone but keep it hidden because you think it would seem too strange and, instead, go with your partner or a friend. Some introverts like to have companionship on a trip. Others prefer to travel alone like Carsten in the example below.

• • • • • • • • • • • •

I love travelling alone. So, I can give myself entirely to enjoying nature, the church, or the concert without needing to converse during it or in some other way earmarking a part of my attention to my travel companion. When I travel alone, I can go right where I want when I want and at my own tempo. It is not because there is no one who wants to come along. But ever since my first solo trip, I have always preferred to travel alone.

Carsten, age 55

• • • • • • • • • • • •

Even though introverts are not typically enthused by others' spontaneous whims or last-minute changes in plans, we like having the opportunity to be spontaneous and to decide, day by day, what we would like to do.

If you have the desire but have never tried to travel alone, perhaps you should give yourself that experience. At the same time, you can treat it as an exercise in letting yourself be guided from within instead of navigating by what others think must be the ideal vacation for you.

Search yourself every time you make a choice: whether you are assessing it from what others think, or whether you have the courage to choose what feels right on the inside – even though others might think it is a strange choice.

Pretending to be someone else
– and the price you pay

Perhaps you have feigned having a feeling that would please another person – for example, when you open a present while the giver watches. You have probably experienced hiding a feeling of irritation or some other negative feeling if, for instance, you get unexpected guests at an inconvenient time. Perhaps you have also experienced pretending to find a speech interesting even though you are bored – or trying to hide how tired you are and, instead, acting like you are as alert as everyone else.

An introverted client confided in me one day the following.

I've often been told that I look grumpy. So, now, I make sure I smile all the time when I'm with other people.

Cecilie, age 24

Being able to smile even though you are not happy is a good skill to have. A smile is also a signal that says, 'You are okay, and I am kindly disposed.' But it is all too stressful to hold a smile for an extended period of time. So, it is better to use your energy on keeping in touch with yourself, so you can express what seems true and right for yourself.

When my grandchild receives a present, she likes to put a blanket over her head while she opens it. I think she does what many of us want to: hide her face so she does not need to strain to show the expression the giver expects.

Trying to be something other than what you are demands an incredible amount of energy, and a reckoning often results afterwards in the form of exhaustion.

Why do we not always show the face that is the true reflection of our feelings at the relevant moment? Why do we not just let our faces relax or look away when we are tired or bored? First of all, we would like to avoid conflicts, clashes, or a bad atmosphere. We also do not like hurting other people's feelings. Many of us also sense very clearly what our interlocutor can handle – and keep to ourselves what lies outside the listener's capacity. We do this not only out of kindness but also because it is unpleasant to reveal something true or talk about something important to someone who can neither handle nor understand it.

This attunement to the person you are with can take place entirely automatically. It is not certain you yourself realise that you have closed down parts of yourself that you sense the other person cannot deal with or understand. Others may not think you have something on your mind. But you probably do. And when you are together with 'peers', you can probably be inspired to talk about things you did not even realise you knew.

If you are very affected by those you are with, it becomes extra important for you to choose your friends with care and not spend too much time with people with whom you do not feel comfortable being who you are. You are probably familiar with the fact that it can be hard to say 'No, thank you' to what most people believe you agree with as a matter of course.

I often experience clients who have a bad conscience about saying no to one social event or another just because they did not have the energy. 'Why can't I just say yes happily and enjoy the company like everybody else?', they typically ask themselves. Here, I pose another question to them that I find far more relevant: 'Why do you want to be a part of an event when you don't feel like it?' The person in question may have different reasons for this. For example, they might like to please the person who offered the invitation. Sometimes, that is the only reason he or she has a bad conscience. In that case, I recommend that they work on dealing with their bad conscience instead of spending their precious time with people who sap their energy.

If, as an introvert or sensitive person, you have adapted yourself according to how those around you think you should be or act, you will suffer severely from it because, then, you are so far from your natural element. You have the opportunity to achieve a high degree of inner freedom to be yourself in your own way. First of all, it is natural for you to direct your focus inward and find a point of orientation when, for example, you make important decisions. Second, it is important for your well-being to keep in touch with yourself. And, third, you probably enjoy being alone and, therefore, are not so dependent on the company of others.

If people around you do not like for you to go your own way and, perhaps, reject you on this basis, you will survive and even do well with only a few friends and, correspondingly, more time alone. It is not 'alone time' that makes us feel lonely. The worst feeling of loneliness arises when we have abandoned ourselves and let ourselves be guided by others' opinions instead of believing in our own attitudes and values.

It is especially important for introverts and sensitive people to live in harmony with themselves and their values. We are not very good at repressing the discomfort in taking another's paths instead of our own. Therefore, it is also important that we do not let a bad conscience drag us around by the nose.

Do not be directed by a bad conscience

Not everyone is familiar with having a bad conscience. Psychopaths, for instance, are not.

A bad conscience may be what gets us to apologise, for example if we have forgotten a birthday, or have come too late for or have missed an appointment. In these instances, a bad conscience is appropriate to the situation and can be fixed with an apology or, perhaps, an offer to make amends.

A bad conscience comes from the idea that you have done something wrong either in your own or another's eyes. It may be correct. Below is an example from my own life.

....

A man with a foreign appearance was standing in line in front of me. He was short 5 euro. I wanted to give him the money, but it felt awkward, and I did not have the energy to be outgoing at that moment. Afterwards, I felt guilty. I had not acted in accordance with my values. But I wanted to.

....

In the example above, a bad conscience is appropriate to the situation. It reminds me that it would be a good thing to improve in this area. Below is another example in which a bad conscience is out of proportion.

....

Susanne has taken sick leave from stress and has been told that her most important task in the coming weeks is to take care of herself. But her family, which was used to her solving problems for them, has a hard time understanding that she just cannot take care of the children for a single day or buy a present when she is not at work anyway. When she says she does not have the energy, they become short-tempered and quickly say goodbye.

Susanne has a bad conscience and many concerns about how her family is dealing with her rebuffs. God forbid that they feel let down or angry, or say something bad about her, so others will think she is not interested in anyone but herself.

She knows the best thing for everyone in the long run is for her to say no to what she does not

have the energy for, so she can get over her stress,
get better again, and once again be able to provide
a helping hand gladly. But her bad conscience and
worries will not leave her in peace. So, she decides
to go out and buy the present since she cannot relax
at home anyway.

In the example above, Susanne allows herself to be
controlled by her guilt. Her illness could have given
her family a chance to learn to take more responsibility
for themselves. But because she cannot stand her bad
conscience, she winds up doing something that puts a
strain on her and benefits no one over the long term.

Some sensitive or introverted people are inclined
to have a bad conscience that is out of proportion. If
they do not succeed at being the perfect son, daughter,
mother, or father, they chastise themselves.

A bad conscience is sometimes the same thing as
anxiety about someone else's anger, and an apology
actually often means 'avoid-punishment', which
means, 'Don't punish me for my offence.' Pay attention
to how often your bad conscience is actually a fear
that others will direct negative feelings toward you.

If you have a hard time dealing with other people's
negative feelings and, therefore, also your own bad
conscience, you might do anything to keep someone
from holding something against you. Perhaps you
use a strategy in which you put your mistake-finder
glasses on and become very attentive to your tiniest
imperfection – in the hope that you can improve on it
before others see it. Perhaps you try to become exactly

what you think those around you want you to be. You hope this strategy may help you avoid the unpleasant feeling of a bad conscience. But, instead, it can both become a vicious circle that can lead to over-exertion and mean that, ultimately, you will have less to give than if you had been able to relax more.

The problem is not the bad conscience but what you do to get rid of it. If you are always on your toes, trying to live up to others' expectations, you can over-exert yourself and, perhaps, forget entirely who you are inside and what you want deep down.

Perhaps you do what Klaus does in the example below.

· · · · · · · · · · · · ·

Sometimes, I set aside a day exclusively to myself. I look forward to it long in advance. I've often planned a walk in the woods or a lot of time just to mess around in my flat, while I listen to my favourite music. On a day like that, it happens sometimes that my adult daughter calls and asks whether I could go into town and buy something for her. My whole body screams NO, but I still say yes because otherwise I'll have a bad conscience.

Klaus, age 58

· · · · · · · · · · · · ·

You can go against your own wishes and needs if it feels meaningful to you or if you would like to please someone else whose need is more pressing than your own. But if you neglect yourself exclusively to avoid a bad conscience, it can become a vicious circle in which you get farther and farther away from being true to yourself, which ends up exhausting you. In addition, you give others a springboard over your boundaries.

You can work with a bad conscience in the same way you work with anxiety. In the cognitive treatment of anxiety, clients learn to expose themselves to what they are afraid of. This is called exposure therapy. When you work with exposure therapy in the treatment of anxiety, you stop trying to avoid what makes you afraid. Instead, you expose yourself to more and more of it until you grow used to it. You can also do this with a bad conscience.

If, instead of cancelling his own plans in the example above, Klaus had said to his daughter that he could not help that day because he had another appointment (with himself), he might get a bad conscience – and, perhaps, his day would be ruined because he worried about what his daughter would think of him. But what if he rehearsed dealing with a bad conscience and got those around him used to the fact that he himself has needs that are important? In addition, what if he shows himself that he can mark out and stick to his own boundaries, which increases his self-worth? The next time he decides to say no to something, it will probably be easier for him.

If, instead of hurrying to give an apology or jumping about to fulfil others' desires and expectations, you decide to follow your own values, others may be disappointed in you at first, and you may have a bad conscience. But, then, you can say to yourself,

'I may have a bad conscience now. But nothing has come from it. I will try to get used to this feeling, so it becomes possible for me to prioritise what seems right for me instead of what everyone else would prefer.'

Be guided by your own values

It is best if you are, first and foremost, guided by your own values. These values may deal with, for example, truth, love, concern for the frail in our society, the environment, fidelity, or freedom.

Finding and living your values and becoming clear about how you would like to live your life are important. Maybe you would like to become better and better at being loving and accommodating to most people. Perhaps you think it is important to be brave enough to reveal yourself and be present in a close and authentic way without any attempt at manipulation or dissimulation. Perhaps, for example, you have a talent for sports, painting, or music which is important for you to cultivate. Perhaps your children's welfare is the most important thing of all.

Speak to someone about your values and make sure they are realistic. If, for instance, it is important to you to be a person everyone likes, you will quickly be working overtime. If you are average, about 80 per cent of the people you meet will like you, while 20 per cent will not.

It may be a good idea to write down your values, perhaps even in order of priority. When you have to make a choice in which following your own values will result in others being disappointed in you, reading through a list of your values can strengthen the side of you that finds it important to be true and faithful to yourself.

An example may be if you decline a social event in order, instead, to collect for the Red Cross. Perhaps, afterwards, you worry what others will think of your decision. Then, it may be a good idea to take out the piece of paper or a book listing your values to remind yourself how important it is for you to make a positive difference for those who need it most.

Below is an example of a prioritised values list.

. . . .

Karen's values:

- Be there for my children.

- Create something with my hands (make sculptures).

- Be with my siblings and parents.

- Be good at my job.

- Be a decent person – honest, real, dependable.

Karen's sister has invited her to a town fair. Karen has a hard time deciding whether to go. On one hand, her sister would like her to join, and she would like to please her sister. On the other hand, she does not much feel like it. When she looks at her list of values, her decision becomes easier.

She declines and earmarks the day for working on her sculptures. This makes her happy and satisfied – and she will have a greater surplus for her

children. Karen's sister is sad that Karen does not
want to go, which gives Karen a bad conscience.
But she sticks to her decision.

Standing up for yourself even when you feel or want
to do something other than what is expected can be a
source of deep satisfaction in life.

Show your difference

Many highly sensitive people and some introverts
have an inclination only to express agreement. We
like to say, 'Yes, I know,' or 'That's how I feel, too.'
On the other hand, we do not always say when we
actually feel differently or simply do not understand
or recognise what the other person is saying. This
inclination toward conformity (we pretend we agree or
believe the same thing) can be a pretext for inaction.
We avoid feeling our difference – and, perhaps, avoid
feeling our anxiety that we are too different or strange
for anyone to want to be with us.

But it is precisely this difference that makes each
of us into a unique human being. The more you
dare to stand up for yourself, the more you step into
character as the unique person you are and the greater
the chances are for you to have a deeply satisfying
experience of being seen and accepted exactly the
way you are.

The more you dare to show who you are – also
when you feel, think, or want something different

from those you are with – the more enriching, educational, and interesting your contact with others will become.

If it feels dangerous or, maybe, just uncomfortable to say that you are not always in agreement with others, you can begin by practising with small things. Below is an easy exercise – and you can find more yourself.

> Ask someone what their favourite colour is. Then, tell them that your taste is different with respect to colours. If she prefers green, perhaps you prefer blue.

The more you practise expressing a different opinion, the more natural it will become.

One day, you may get the courage to express your differences in a major, important area and, for example, tell your mother, or some other significant person, that there is an area in her image of you that is not in agreement with your own. Then, account for the difference between the way she sees you and the way you experience yourself. When you do that, you will probably experience a strong feeling of stepping into character.

> Most of my life I've been absorbed with being 'right', so I could avoid feeling like an outsider or being criticised. I kept hidden – as far as possible, from others and from myself – those sides of my character from which others might distance themselves.

> When I began to dare to show more and more
> of myself, social interaction became easier and
> more fun.
>
> *Hanne, age 40*

Standing up for yourself is pretty much the same as standing up for your everyday desires in life.

Express your wishes with dignity

When you give expression to a desire, it makes a difference whether you use the expression 'need' or 'would like'. In the first instance, you put greater pressure on the other person because 'need' approaches saying 'can't live without'.

If, for example, you would like the other person to give you a kiss but only if he or she wants to, you must put the least-possible pressure on them and, therefore, avoid saying, 'I need a kiss,' but instead say, 'I would like a kiss.'

Let us take another example: you have a hard time working when others are talking on the phone near you. You decide to go to your boss with the problem. Should you say, 'I need some peace,' or, 'I would like to have some peace'? It depends on how brave you are and how amenable your boss is. If you say 'need', you do not take nearly as much responsibility for the problem. You cannot help what you need. If you are really incapable of working when you are surrounded by noise, it is not wrong. The risk that you will get a 'no' is probably less if you use the expression 'need'. Still, it is far more dignified to use the expression 'would like'. Here, you are not a victim of your own needs but someone who wants something particular. If it is a case of being unable to work with that level of noise, it must appear that this is an important piece of information for your boss.

As a rule of thumb, 'need' can be considered when you are together with people in a situation in which you have to fight to be seen and accepted as you are and where you have not experienced the other person as being especially willing to give you what you want. Here, it may be a good idea to put a little extra pressure on.

On the other hand, if you are with people in a situation in which it is possible to have loving, authentic contact, 'would like' is the formulation that allows the other person freely and gladly to give you what you want – or not.

Some introverts or highly sensitive people feel so insecure (when they have to express a wish or a need that is different from the majority's) that they think they should explain or apologise for being the way they are. Perhaps they try to explain that they are introverts or highly sensitive. Not that this is always wrong, but be aware that it often provides more respect if you just say what you want or do not want – without apologising or explaining. Here are a couple of examples:

~ 'I am glad you thought of inviting me, but unfortunately I have to decline coming to your reception, because I am highly sensitive and…'

~ 'Receptions are not really my cup of tea, so I regretfully decline but am glad you thought of inviting me.'

In the first example, the rejection of the reception is explained by personality type. In some cases, this can be a good solution. But I personally think that it is far more dignified and shows more self-respect simply by saying what you would prefer – or do not care for.

Others make do with a white lie, as in the example below.

I recently moved to Vendsyssel to be with my boyfriend. Here, in the countryside, it does not feel natural for me to say that I'm over-stimulated. So I'll just say I have a stomach ache when I need to come home early from a party.

Irene, age 58

Irene could instead decide to explain what it is to be an introvert and, thus, give an honest reason for going home early. She could also just say she is tired and wants to go home, but it might make those who remain wonder whether she thought something was wrong with the party. A white lie is sometimes the least complicated for all parties.

Chapter 7

Find a Refuge in Regarding Yourself as an Introvert or Highly Sensitive Person

Perhaps others have suggested to you that you work on becoming a little faster on the uptake, and more spontaneous and sociable – or, in some other way, have let you know that it would be better if you behaved more like an extrovert than it feels natural for you to do so. In that case, you have probably also found a huge joy of recognition when you heard about your type and, perhaps, slowly began to find the courage to stand up for yourself and find peace in being who you are and to discover that others feel the same as you. It can be like finding a foothold in the midst of confusion and stress; like finding a refuge where you are allowed to be what you are and you can be protected from the pressure and well-meaning advice of others about how you should change.

Paradoxically, this peace gives us the reserves to investigate whether we can come to terms with some of our challenges. When others stop challenging us, we sometimes have the desire to challenge ourselves, like Maria in the following example.

> For many years, my family and my partner tried to convince me that I should do something to learn to think more positively about myself. But it did not make sense to me, and I was irritated that they wanted to change me. When I discovered I was an introvert, a lot of pieces fell into place. I asked those close to me to read about introversion – and they could also see it and came to understand me better. And my negative thoughts about myself faded.
>
> Once a couple of years had gone by after this new recognition – 'I am OK as I am and do not need to change' – I got the desire to investigate whether something could be changed. I wanted to be able to feel myself as one of the crowd at my workplace to a greater extent. One day, I was so motivated that I threw myself into it with my heart and soul and tried a number of things, including alternative treatments and psychotherapy. I can't say what it was that helped, but today I enjoy being with my colleagues to a higher degree.
>
> *Maria, age 38*

No one has a desire to change or develop because others think it might be a good idea. It is hard work, and it can also provoke anxiety. Because who am I, then? If something needs to be changed or developed, you have to be highly motivated and have plenty of energy reserves.

Recognising yourself as belonging to a personality type can provide you with these reserves. You can profitably shift between periods in which you are resting and accept yourself and your situation as it is, and other periods in which you work at developing yourself.

The serenity of knowing your type should preferably not become an eternal rest or a form of stagnation. Every new age or life situation has its opportunities and challenges and requires you to relate to yourself and, perhaps, learn to handle what you are struggling with in new ways. If every time you run into an obstacle, you think, 'My obstacle is due to the fact that I am an introvert or highly sensitive person, so I have to learn to live with it,' you risk missing out on the growth opportunities life offers. Nothing is completely static. We develop throughout life. The problems that cannot be solved at one age of life might be changed in the next.

What can be treated?

It can be difficult to assess what can be worked on and what must be accepted as a condition of life. I like this wise prayer of unknown origin:

> God, grant me the serenity to accept the things
> I cannot change,
> Courage to change the things I can,
> And wisdom to know the difference.

It is a shame if you struggle with problems that can be alleviated with psychotherapy and you do not seek out the right help.

In my practice as a therapist, I sometimes find that clients are afraid their problems are far too small to allow themselves to take up my time. Often, I think it is a shame that the person in question had not come ten years earlier. Many people carry around painful secrets or burdensome self-images for far too long before they seek help.

Many highly sensitive people and some introverts have negative thoughts about themselves. In the personality types themselves, there is a slight inclination to see oneself through critical eyes because we would prefer to discover flaws before others do. But if your everyday mood is burdened by negative thoughts about yourself or if you are tired and sad for an extended period of time, you may have depression.

If you feel socially restricted by anxiety about others' negative thoughts about you or about being an embarrassment so that you lie awake half the night and chastise yourself for relatively small flaws or offences, you may have a degree of social anxiety. Both depression and anxiety can profitably be treated with psychotherapy.

If you are having a hard time getting your relationships to function satisfactorily, it may be, for example, because you have unprocessed sorrow in your baggage or trauma that may be more burdensome than you can even remember.

If you are extremely afraid, for instance of the anger of others, you should be aware that you may have PTSD. If you do not remember it, ask your parents whether you were subjected to violence when you were a child. It does not have to have been life-threatening, but perhaps you experienced it that way and that is enough to give rise to serious trauma. Perhaps your parents beat you as part of your upbringing or, you had violent siblings or experienced something in the playground you thought was life-threatening.

If you have experiences in your past that you can barely stand to think about, it is a good idea to talk to someone about it. If you are in doubt, then try to describe the situation to someone else. If tears flow, that is fine. But if you are devastated and have a hard time containing yourself and your feelings, it is probably something that needs to be looked at more closely.

As a starting point, we would all prefer to talk about a good childhood with competent parents. It can take a long time to reach an acknowledgment of the anxiety and pain that must have been there or of the failings of a parent. Therefore, many people continue to be convinced that their childhood was entirely good even though they never dare to scratch the surface and investigate whether this presumption holds water under close investigation, as in the example below.

> I have always told myself that I had a good, safe childhood. Seen in hindsight, I understand now that, in my family, we actually looked down on those who had a troubled upbringing. I had an aunt about whom my father said that she was downright neurotic – this was because she had had a bad childhood. I was glad I didn't belong to my aunt's category.
>
> Later in life, however, I had to acknowledge that there were also experiences in my childhood that had made me into a person who is sometimes difficult or who over-reacts.
>
> When I look back now on my aunt with my own – and not my father's – eyes, I understand that she might have reacted nervously or inappropriately in certain situations but that, in other situations, she could act with a depth and a wisdom that not many people have. She had had to dive deeper into the mysteries of existence to find meaning – and it had given her a greater understanding of the suffering of others and an ability to listen and understand. Today, I would claim that I'm like her.
>
> *Inger, age 61*

Looking more closely at your own history and discovering new things about your parents and yourself can be both fun and interesting. It can also become a journey through anxiety and grief. But the road ahead can provide new, life-improving insights and knowledge.

If you lacked support in your childhood, you can as an adult learn to support and acknowledge yourself. If you practise and become good at self-love, you break the vicious circle. If your parents were unable to give you the right support, it was probably because they did not get the right support from their parents, who again did not get the right support from their parents. This kind of incompetence can go back many generations. It only takes one eager, persistent person to break this social legacy – and if you do it, it will pass positive results down through the generations.

Some people decline help even though they are struggling with huge problems because they are afraid the therapist will want to change them. It also happens that therapists try to get introverts or sensitive people to become more spontaneous or extroverted than is natural for them. If that is the case, it is a matter of finding another therapist. Psychologists and psychotherapists all have their strengths and weaknesses. Do not reject all psychotherapy just because you tried a single psychotherapist whom you do not feel was of any help to you. The right support can make life easier, as the example below illustrates.

Before I became good at asking for help, my life was unnecessarily harsh. I once saw in a dream an image of a dogged, cowled person, who was struggling through darkness, rain, and wind. That's what my life was like for periods at a time. Now, I've become good at asking for help and seeking shelter and warmth with other people.

Agnete, age 48

Chapter 8

Use Precise, Neutral Language about Yourself

The language that is often used about introverts or highly sensitive people needs to be corrected. You may find yourself using a language about yourself that is negative and imprecise. It may be something you have heard others say about you and you have accepted it uncritically. Below are a number of examples.

Social – but not always sociable

Some sensitive or introverted people say about themselves that they are not social. But they probably are. They just have not learned the distinction between being social and being sociable.

Being sociable means wanting company.

Being social means thinking of the community and the welfare of others as well as your own.

Extroverts are more sociable than introverts.

Both can be more or less social. Introverts may be uninterested in others, and extroverts sometimes forget in their eagerness to talk to make room for others to speak: two different ways of being less social.

Elaine Aron believes that, as a starting point, highly sensitive people think very socially. They often ask themselves, 'If everyone acted the way I do, how would the world look?' – and, of course, they would like to be able to answer that the world would look like a nice place to be.

You can be social without being sociable. For example, it can be a very social decision to decline attending a party in order to save your energy for your family the next day.

Self-examination – not self-absorption

Highly sensitive and introverted people are sometimes viewed as self-absorbed because they think about themselves a lot.

But, actually, they are examining themselves, which is to say that, if anyone is not thriving around them, they will quickly look to themselves and ask, 'Is any of this negativity my fault? And how can I help make it nice for everyone?'

If everyone were equally thorough in examining themselves, the world would see fewer wars and conflicts.

Low threshold of pain – not whining

Many sensitive people have been told that they whine and should pull themselves together. But when you have a lower threshold of pain and a sensitive nervous system, you are more sensitive to cold and warmth, for example – and you cannot just pull yourself together and pretend nothing is wrong.

Extra sensitive – not over-sensitive

Many people have been called 'over-sensitive' as if they had too much of something. It is correct that we can be very sensitive, but it is not too much. People are born with different degrees of sensitivity – or acquire greater sensitivity through life experiences. No one is too much or too little of something. Each of us is okay exactly as we are.

Recharging or in energy-saving mode – not lazy

Very energetic people sometimes consider us to be lazy when we move slowly or do very little. But we are probably in our energy-saving mode or simply recharging.

Different – not wrong

As introverts or highly sensitive people, we simply function differently from the majority. There can be advantages to being different. I myself am comfortable with this. If I were utterly ordinary, not that many people would want to read my books.

A dislike of fighting – not necessarily an inability to express anger

Some sensitive or introverted people have been told that it would be good for them to express their anger better. But our reticence to enter into conflicts is rarely due to our inability to feel our anger or our inability to express it. We just prefer dialogue and negotiation – and, sometimes, choose to be flexible because we do not care for conflicts and would rather use our energy on something else.

Both strong – and delicate

Some people view us as delicate. I personally feel comfortable with using the word 'delicate' about myself. It makes me think of silk and butterflies. But others connect being delicate with being weak. If that is what you think, it is probably not a word you would use about yourself. We typically have strong ethical views, deeply held opinions, original ideas, and a well-developed sense of empathy.

Well-considered – not boring

Some people may think that we are boring because, in some contexts, we do not say much. But it is not because we have not thought about things or have no opinion or have nothing on our minds. We just do not like fighting to have our say. Moreover, we are very much aware of whether what we are thinking about saying benefits the other person, ourselves, or the community. We do not need to say something just to say something. We would rather hold our tongue if we are uncertain about whether what we are thinking about saying is important to the other person.

Limited energy resources – not snobbish or arrogant

We are sometimes viewed as snobbish or arrogant when we avoid contact. Often, we are just over-stimulated or deeply engaged in thinking about or developing ideas. So, we do not want to be disturbed by social contact.

Since our energy for sociability is limited, we have to engage in a strict prioritisation with respect to whom we spend time with. If we are to thrive, we need time for recharging and creative pleasures or experiences in nature, for example.

Another kind of courage – not, for example, a wimp

The opposite of being a wimp is being a hero. Our conception of a hero often has to do with big muscles – a strong man who throws himself into dangerous situations to save someone. But I also think that it is an aspect of being a hero if you struggle to be a good father or mother despite too little sleep or alone time, and if you admit your flaws and apologise when it is necessary. Courage is daring to recognise your own limitations too, and coming to terms with both your weaknesses and strengths.

Sometimes focused on the self – not egocentric

It is especially important for introverted and sensitive people to keep in touch with their deeper layers, what C.G. Jung called 'the self'. It is here we can also have contact with the divine, our guardian spirit, the spirit of God, or whatever you want to call the spiritual dimension that many of us find important to keep in contact with throughout life. It is also here that we look ourselves in the eyes and figure out whether we are on the right path. Being an introvert is not the same thing as being a navel-gazer who is only interested in his or her own concerns. On the contrary, many of us have a well-developed ethical sense and values that are particularly directed toward the welfare of others.

Interested in other people's well-being
– not necessarily in hearing about their
deeds or listening to their stories

We are not typically that interested in the deeds or accomplishments of other people. But we are often very interested in how other people are.

We take things seriously – not too seriously

Many sensitive or introverted people have been told that they should stop taking things so seriously.

I myself take things and people very seriously and often also literally. It took me many years to learn that, when people ask, 'How are you?', it is not certain they are interested in a long, careful answer. And when people wrote 'Hope you are well', I believed they were worried on my behalf and I felt obliged to calm them with an extended account of how I was doing in spite of everything. Now I have learned that, most of the time, you just say, 'Fine, thanks,' and 'Hope you're well, too.' But I spend two seconds considering whether the person who is asking is an introvert or a sensitive person because, if that is the case, the person probably means it seriously and literally and would like to hear something personal and honest from me.

Another time I have noticed that I take what people say too much at face value is if a person – perhaps, just in passing – mentions that the room is cold. Then, I immediately look to see whether there is a window I can close or a radiator I can turn up, and consider whether I should offer the person my sweater. But, sometimes, it turns out that the person just said something about the temperature in order to say something or other to get the conversation rolling.

Highly sensitive and introverted people can enjoy taking life a bit easier. But think how many accidents could have been prevented if everyone took all the problems of the world equally seriously. Then, just think how many economic crises or environmental catastrophes could have been avoided.

Sensitive and Introverted People Are Starting to Insist on Being in the World in Their Own Way

Over the past two decades, there has been great interest in learning about different personality traits or types and, particularly, in finding out where one belongs. Highly sensitive and introverted people form groups online and on social media – and, sometimes, also in real life. Here, they enjoy finding reflections of themselves and share advice and strategies to deal with the challenge of living in a culture that assesses extroversion – for example, the desire to be sociable – as worth more than the desire to think deeply or to be comfortable alone.

It is my impression that introverted and highly sensitive people have gained the courage to struggle longer before they leave a job, for example. The shame over acting differently from most others has diminished for many. So, instead of quitting a job in which they are not thriving, they have become more inclined to talk to their bosses about what is bothering them – and, perhaps, even with a boss higher up in the hierarchy if they do not feel they have been understood by the first one.

Many introverts, however, continue to be afraid to stand up for their type publicly because they fear it will damage their chances in the labour market. But more and more are beginning to embrace their introversion or sensitivity, to straighten their backs, and to assert themselves more by contributing their thoughts and ideas. I think this is a good development for the world. Introverts and highly sensitive people are good at imagining new possibilities and solutions to problems, large and small. They also have a talent for predicting what can go wrong, and they no longer let themselves be brushed aside with remarks such as 'You should look positively at things' and 'Don't go looking for trouble.'

When people choose to embrace their inherent character and stand up for themselves as introverts or highly sensitive people, they become models for others. The rings, then, spread out in the water so that more and more people take their place in the community with self-confidence – without hiding or being ashamed.

I hope and believe that this development will continue: that introverts and highly sensitive people will become better and better at setting boundaries and organising their lives, so they can thrive and the world can benefit from their talents. That there will come greater and greater understanding in the world for the idea that all people have equal worth whether they are sensitive or robust, men or women, regardless of what land or what conditions they come from. And that fear of people who are different will be replaced by an acknowledgment that people can be – and act – very differently and still be okay exactly as they are.

Test Yourself

Below are two tests I have developed for this book. In the first, you can test your relative introversion or extroversion and, in the second, your sensitivity.

How introverted or extroverted are you?

Place a number after each statement. You have five different possible answers.

0 = Does not fit me

1 = Fits me a little

2 = Somewhat fits me

3 = Almost fits me

4 = Fits me well

1. I prefer peace and quiet to being where a lot of activities are going on around me _____

2. When words are flowing at a brisk tempo, and we challenge each other in a discussion, I am in my element _____

3. I am selectively sociable. In some contexts and together with certain people, I enjoy company very much, but otherwise I prefer to be alone to being with others _____

4. I like going to big receptions with plenty of opportunities to meet new people _____

5. Other people have told me I am too reticent _____

6. I take things as they come and rarely worry too much _____

7. Small talk exhausts me _____

8. I do not need to think things through before I say something. It comes to me as I talk _____

9. I don't like to have onlookers while I work _____

10. If too little is going on around me, I get a little tired. Then, I need company to boost my energy again _____

11. When I am going to a party, I prefer to
     know in advance what will happen at the
     party. Of course, there must be room for
     spontaneity, but I like to know in broad
     strokes what is going to happen   _____

12. I like throwing myself unprepared into
     new experiences   _____

13. For the most part, I speak in quiet, calm
     tones and only rarely raise my voice   _____

14. I do a lot to keep myself from being bored
     and try to have too many rather than too
     few appointments or activities on my
     calendar   _____

15. My knowledge is deeper than it is broad.
     I know a lot about one or a few topics,
     but there are many other areas where my
     knowledge is lacking   _____

16. I am often among the last to go home
     from a party   _____

17. If I have absorbed a lot of impressions,
     I need to be alone to think about them   _____

18. I derive energy from activities and social
     interactions and rarely become tired as
     long as what is happening around me is
     sufficiently interesting   _____

19. Others have told me that I think too much
    about things   _____

20. I am rarely passive when I am with a
    communicative group of people. Even
    among people I do not know, I quickly
    seize the chance to involve myself in the
    conversation   _____

21. If my own experience of what is true
    and correct conflicts with the common
    understanding of what is good, I am
    inclined to listen more to my own logic or
    intuition   _____

22. I easily fall into conversation with people
    I do not know – for example, at a bus stop _____

23. It is important for me to have time alone
    to myself every day   _____

24. Every so often, I become so inspired that
    I cannot keep my opinion to myself even
    though someone else is saying something   _____

25. It is somewhat straining for me to relate to
    several people at once   _____

26. I am very aware of and interested in the
    activities that go on around me – so much
    so, I can overlook my own needs, for
    example for food or sleep   _____

27. If, on my birthday, I am among people
    other than those close to me (for example,
    on a course) I hope no one discovers it
    because I don't like being the centre of
    attention on that occasion   _____

28. I would be happy to suddenly discover
    that I was going to a surprise party
    that my friends had arranged for me to
    celebrate something for which I had not
    found time to arrange a celebration myself _____

29. I prefer one-on-one conversations as
    opposed to conversations in larger groups   _____

30. I adapt myself quickly to a new group and
    follow naturally the train of thought in a
    new context   _____

31. I am inclined to listen to my inner feelings
    and intuition for an answer to something
    instead of finding the answers outside
    myself   _____

32. I like hearing the sound of other people
    and their activities and would rather have
    too much going on around me than too
    much quiet   _____

Statements with odd numbers constitute group 1. Statements with even numbers constitute group 2.

Group 1   ## Group 2

Statement 1 _____   Statement 2 _____

Statement 3 _____   Statement 4 _____

Statement 5 _____   Statement 6 _____

Statement 7 _____   Statement 8 _____

Statement 9 _____   Statement 10 _____

Statement 11 _____   Statement 12 _____

Statement 13 _____   Statement 14 _____

Statement 15 _____   Statement 16 _____

Statement 17 _____   Statement 18 _____

Statement 19 _____   Statement 20 _____

Statement 21 _____   Statement 22 _____

Statement 23 _____   Statement 24 _____

Statement 25 _____   Statement 26 _____

Statement 27 _____   Statement 28 _____

Statement 29 _____   Statement 30 _____

Statement 31 _____   Statement 32 _____

Sum group 1 _59_   **Sum group 2** _19_

Add all the numbers in both groups together. If, for example, you have answered 1 to all the statements in group 1, the sum for this group is 16. If, for instance, you have answered 2 to every statement, the sum here is 32.

Take the sum of group 1 and subtract the sum of group 2. Then, you have a number for your introversion or extroversion. (For example, if your number for group 1 is 28, and your number for group 2 is 14, your number will be 28 − 14 = 14.)

Sum of group 1 = _____

Sum of group 2 = _____

Group 1 sum minus group 2 sum = _____

The number will lie somewhere between minus 64 and plus 64. The higher your number is, the more introverted or (if the number is negative) extroverted you are. If your number is around 0, you are an ambivert.

When you have found your number, you can locate yourself on the scale below.

−60 −50 −40 −30 −20 −10   0   10   20   30   40   50   60

Extrovert   Ambivert   Introvert

How sensitive are you?

Place a number after each statement. You have five different possible answers.

0 = Does not fit me

1 = Fits me a little

2 = Somewhat fits me

3 = Almost fits me

4 = Fits me

1. I spend more energy than most people on trying to foresee what might go wrong and then take precautions   4

2. I think a brisk fight is refreshing   1

3. If I receive too many impressions, I need to be alone to think about them   4

4. For the most part, I am energetic and in a good mood almost regardless of what is going on around me   2,

5. I easily get a bad conscience   4

6. Social interaction does not tire me. If the atmosphere is good, I can enjoy it from morning to night without needing to withdraw to be alone or rest   0

7. I can be very irritated by light, smells, and sounds that do not seem to bother most other people   2

8. I take things as they come and rarely worry very much

0

9. If I am too cold or too warm, I cannot ignore it but have to change the temperature or go somewhere else

4

10. I like to throw myself unprepared into new experiences

0

11. I prefer dialogues with intimacy, depth, or meaning to small talk

4

12. I like working under pressure

1

13. If I happen to behave awkwardly with someone else and the person in question is upset about it, I feel very guilty and am powerfully affected by it for a while

4

14. I think people who are doing poorly have mostly themselves to blame

0

15. When I see someone doing unpleasant work, for example digging with a shovel in stifling heat or working in noisy surroundings without ear protection, I feel bad myself

4

16. I sleep heavily and well at night and am not disturbed by either light or sound

0

17. I am easily inspired and get many good ideas

4

18. I feel no need to interfere with how others treat their pets. It is their responsibility, not mine _____2_____

19. I like being surrounded by stillness in nature _____4_____

20. I eat pretty much everything and am neither delicate nor picky _____'2_____

Statements with odd numbers constitute group 1. Statements with even numbers constitute group 2.

Group 1

Statement 1 _____

Statement 3 _____

Statement 5 _____

Statement 7 _____

Statement 9 _____

Statement 11 _____

Statement 13 _____

Statement 15 _____

Statement 17 _____

Statement 19 _____

Sum group 1 _____

Group 2

Statement 2 _____

Statement 4 _____

Statement 6 _____

Statement 8 _____

Statement 10 _____

Statement 12 _____

Statement 14 _____

Statement 16 _____

Statement 18 _____

Statement 20 _____

Sum group 2 _____

Add the numbers to the answers in both groups together. If, for example, you have answered 1 to all statements in group 1, the sum for this group will be 10. If, for instance, you have answered 2 to each statement, the sum here is 20.

Take the sum of group 1 and subtract the sum of group 2. Then, you have a number for your sensitivity. (For example, if your number for group 1 is 9, and your number for group 2 is 11, your number will be $9 - 11 = -2$.)

Sum of group 1 = _____

Sum of group 2 = _____

Group 1 sum minus group 2 sum = _____

The number will lie somewhere between minus 40 and plus 40. The higher your number is, the more sensitive you are. If your number is around 0, you may be moderately sensitive.

When you have found your number, you can locate yourself on the scale below.

−40	−30	−20	−10	0	10	20	30	40

Ordinarily sensitive   Moderately sensitive   Highly sensitive

There is a more comprehensive sensitivity test with 48 statements in my book *Highly Sensitive People in an Insensitive World: How to Create a Happy Life.*

Tests should always be taken with a grain of salt. If you want to learn something about a person from a test, it will never be satisfactory. There are too many aspects that are not included. And the result may well vary depending on your mood or your situation in life on the test day. Let the tests give you an idea of how you function but do not take them for more than they are.

Thanks to...

Registered psychotherapist and Master of Theology Bent Falk, to whom I have had the pleasure of listening in many different contexts over many years.

Thanks, too, to all the sensitive souls I have spoken to in pastoral care or in my practice as a therapist, and to those who have been to my lectures or taken my courses. A special thanks those who have granted me permission to use their stories in this book.

Thanks to MA in Communication Martin Håstrup, introvert.dk, who has repeatedly read and discussed my manuscript with me and given me expert feedback.

Thanks as well for inspirational sparring to Knud Erik Andersen, Margith Christiansen, Kirstin Damgaard, Line Crump Horsted, Janet Cecilie Ligaard, and Kirstine Sand. You have each in your way left your mark on this book.

Bibliography

Aron, E. (1997) *The Highly Sensitive Person.* New York: Broadway Books.

Aron, E. (2001) *The Highly Sensitive Person in Love: Understanding and Managing Relationships When the World Overwhelms You.* New York: Broadway Books.

Aron, E. (2002) *The Highly Sensitive Child: Helping Our Children Thrive When the World Overwhelms Them.* New York: Broadway Books.

Aron, E. (2006) 'The clinical implications of Jung's concept of sensitiveness.' *Journal of Jungian Theory and Practice 8,* 2, 11–43.

Buber, M. (2010) *I and Thou.* Eastford, CT: Martino Fine Books.

Cain, S. (2013) *Quiet: The Power of Introverts in a World That Can't Stop Talking.* London: Penguin.

Falk, B. (2017) *Honest Dialogue: Presence, Common Sense, and Boundaries When You Want to Help Someone.* London: Jessica Kingsley Publishers.

Jung, C.G. (1976) *Psychological Types*. Princeton, NJ: Princeton University Press.

Kagan, J. (1998) *Galen's Prophecy: Temperament in Human Nature.* Boulder, CO: Westview Press.

Kagan, J. and Snidman, N. (2004) *The Long Shadow of Temperament.* Cambridge, MA: Belknap Press of Harvard University Press.

Laney, M.O. (2002) *The Introvert Advantage: How to Thrive in an Extrovert World.* New York: Workman Publishing Company.

Rosenberg, M.B. (2003) *Nonviolent Communication: A Language of Life.* Encinitas, CA: PuddleDancer Press.

Sand, I. (2016) *The Emotional Compass: How to Think Better About Your Feelings.* London: Jessica Kingsley Publishers.

Sand, I. (2016) *Highly Sensitive People in an Insensitive World: How to Create a Happy Life.* London: Jessica Kingsley Publishers.

Sand, I. (2017) *Come Closer: On love and self-protection.* London: Jessica Kingsley Publishers.

Sand, I. (2017) *Tools for Helpful Souls: Especially for highly sensitive people who provide help either on a professional or private level.* London: Jessica Kingsley Publishers.

Yalom, I.D. (1980) *Existential Psychotherapy.* New York: Basic Books.